Bertolt Brecht Poems

Edited by JOHN WILLETT *and* RALPH MANHEIM
with the co-operation of Erich Fried

Part One 1913–1928

LONDON
Eyre Methuen

Contents

THE TRANSLATORS

Edith Anderson · Lee Bremer · John Cullen ·
Michael Hamburger · Frank Jellinek · Lesley Lendrum ·
Peter Levi · H. B. Mallalieu · Christopher Middleton ·
Humphrey Milne · Michael Morley · Edith Roseveare ·
George Rapp · Naomi Replansky · Muriel Rukeyser ·
John Willett · J. F. Williams.

Introduction

It is bad luck that so many of us have been led to approach Brecht from the wrong end: studying the theories first and then the plays, and only coming to the poems as a by-product of his theatre work; instead of seeing that the poems led into and permeated the plays, from which the theories in turn sprang. In part this is due to the unavoidable difficulties of translation, since it is always simpler to translate expository writing than dialogue, while great poetry is ten times harder than even the finest play. Even though Brecht was in some crucial respects unusually close to English literature and the English language, had read much about America and actually spent six years as an exile in the United States, his poetry is still hardly at all known in the English-speaking world.

Yet in reality the translation problem has only been a subsidiary one, since for many years the explosive force of Brecht's poetry was not fully felt even within his own country. It was never easy to get hold of, for a start. Because the Nazis so disapproved of it, his first book virtually disappeared from view within six or seven years of publication, while his second and third were only published in small editions by émigré firms, and could not be brought into the country until after 1945. So long as Brecht himself was alive, in other words, there was scarcely any way for those who had remained in Nazi Germany (or been born there) to study even those poems which he had been willing to publish. And then it turned out that this was only a small proportion of his total poetic output. Out of approximately one thousand items in the collected edition of his poems in 1967 no more than 170 had appeared in the three collections made by himself – and even they included a score or more of songs from the plays. More perhaps than any other major writer except Kafka, Brecht was content that the greater part of his achievement should remain unknown.

Roughly five hundred poems are included in the present volume. Just over a quarter of them were in the three collections, while as much as 64 per cent had (so far as we know) never been published in any form, however ephemeral, before the 1960s, when the first collected edition began to come out in Frankfurt and East Berlin. This staggering indifference to much of his own work was typical of Brecht right through; there were also essays and unfinished plays which he was quite happy to shelve and forget. But he did in a special sense feel that his poetry was private to him.

And so the discovery of Brecht the lyric poet has been a gradual process on all sides. Even the songs and the unrhymed political poetry – which are probably the two most familiar categories of his verse – took time to penetrate to postwar German writers, so much so that their influence in both halves of Germany is still an active one.

Nothing else in Brecht's literary remains can compare with this great mass of previously unknown verse, which has gradually pushed his weight (as it were) away from the theatre towards the poetry shelf. Previously Brecht, for all his evident genius, had seemed a rather limited poet, restricted (whether by choice or by a sense of his own shortcomings) to comparatively few themes and styles. Now it became clear that though the output might ebb and flow, it was limited only in so far as Brecht had decided to publish what was limited (or perhaps merely consistent) about it. This is true of its form as well as its content, for the range of styles which he had at his command was always much wider than he permitted to appear, and nearly always well adapted to the sense and function of the poem in question. His gifts, like his interests, turned out to be unexpectedly rich.

Particularly when Brecht's own arrangements are disregarded and the whole body of poems looked at in chronological order, the pressure of recent German history on the sensitive individual, and through him on the verse, comes to seem overpowering. Thus one sees first how his early sense of sympathy for society's victims and rejects, interlocked with his feeling for the warm south German landscape, is succeeded by the shock of contact with the big city and its granite indifference. Then follows the satirical, more and more political attack on that society and on the Nazis who arrive to take it over, leading after 1933 to an exile which many Germans shared but few could express so tellingly. The screw tightens still further as the Soviet purges of the later 1930s are followed by the Second World War (nowhere more desperately than in 'In times of extreme persecution' p. 351) after which came the American experience with its many frustrations, and then the return to a battered, divided Germany misunderstood by its occupiers and still haunted by Nazi and Stalinist ghosts. It all moves past with a terrible clarity, particularly when the poet is not bothering to make the moral explicit or to suppress his own personal concerns. He was, we can now see, all the time finding the words, the forms and the images for the disastrous history of Germany between the First World War and the aftermath of Stalin's death. More painfully (and in the long run more powerfully) than in any of his stage works, he was writing the tragedy of our time.

*   *   *

Many of the earliest poems were written to be sung to the guitar, like the *Baal* songs which Brecht included in his first collection. Here he was following a tradition established by the Munich playwright Frank Wedekind and maintained by such other performers in that city as the clown Karl Valentin and the sailor-poet Joachim Ringelnatz. 'I was always thinking of actual delivery', says his essay 'On Rhymeless Verse', and indeed it is surprising how many of those poems prove to have still untranscribed melodies in Brecht's quasi-plainchant notation. Though there was also much that he wrote primarily for silent reading – the Psalms, for instance – his characteristic directness and avoidance of ambiguities could always be traced back to the same need: to put the poem across in the most effective possible way.

He found his models in the narrative ballad – at that time a quite unfashionable genre – and the unassuming, genuinely popular (as opposed to folksy) song, no matter how the literary pundits might look down on it. He spurned the arty or artificial folk tradition, as revived by middle-class enthusiasts at the end of the nineteenth century, in favour of the despised pop songs of the same period, such as came to inspire poems like the 'Ballad of the pirates' (p. 18) and 'Remembering Marie A.' (p. 35) with its beautiful slushy tune.

At the same time of course he had his highbrow models, but apart from Wedekind they too came from outside the sanctified corpus of German literature. Villon, who set the pattern for the *Threepenny Opera* songs and is commemorated by two of the poems in our collection, seems to have been known to him by 1918 as a master of the right form and tone for the kind of anarchic, asocial themes that Brecht was beginning to make his own. Whitman he is thought to have discovered while at school; while Rimbaud too he read in German very early on. Both these poets accorded in their own ways with the influence which Brecht himself felt as the strongest of all, that of the Lutheran Bible whose language and themes are time and again echoed in his writings, as, for instance, in his first book of *Devotions* (as we shall call the *Hauspostille*). Not surprisingly then his other great exemplar, even in those early days, was Rudyard Kipling, who not only reflects much the same influences, ranging from the odes of Horace to the Salvationist hymn and the music-hall song, but relates (however unexpectedly by English standards) to the exotic Rimbaud of the 'Bateau ivre'. At that time Brecht so far as we know did not read English, but a volume of Kipling's *Soldatenlieder und andere Gedichte* had appeared in translation in 1910, and he had some acquaintance at least with *Barrack Room Ballads*, *Soldiers Three* and *The Light that Failed* before leaving Munich University in 1921.

A year later the *Devotions* were virtually complete, and Brecht was beginning to be known outside his immediate Augsburg circle as a new voice in German poetry: a mixture of grimness and irony, objectivity and isolation. Up till then the verse had simply poured out of him – all adding up to the single, self-consistent poem whose stage expression was *Baal*. The nation-wide success of his second play *Drums in the Night* broke into this, absorbing Brecht for the first time entirely in the theatre, temporarily blocking his poetic output, then in 1924 luring him to Berlin while all the time putting off the final revision and publication of the *Devotions*. What got him going once more seems to have been a combination of factors: first the failure of the Deutsches Theater in Berlin to give him anything definite to do; then the arrival of a gifted new collaborator in Elisabeth Hauptmann, whose first task was to get the *Devotions* out; above all the impact of the massive Prussian capital, which already on the occasion of his previous visit had shown its power to squeeze the verse out of him in a new gritty form.

By 1926 he had already begun writing the occasional political ballad inspired (like 'Eight thousand poor people assembled outside the city' p. 121) by some item in the news. This was the time of reportage and of Brecht's own collaboration with the documentary theatre of Erwin Piscator, and his growing political interests kept him writing poems even when around 1928–29 his more private inspirations again seemed to dry up. Though the immediate reason was perhaps the sudden success of the *Threepenny Opera*, which kept him fully involved in the theatre during those two years, there were at the same time other pressures in the form of the world economic crisis and the growth of the Nazi movement. Coming to a head in May 1929 shortly before the Wall Street crash (commemorated in 'Late lamented fame of the giant city of New York', p. 167), they did not lead him right into the Communist party, but an extremely close working relationship developed particularly involving the composer Hanns Eisler. Eisler, like the working-class girl Margarete Steffin who became Brecht's main literary aide in the 1930s, was a key influence on his poetic work, for he would not only query its political sense but also make Brecht cut and change for the sake of greater directness or exactitude.

For about the next five years, while the Nazis came to power in Germany and most of Brecht's friends and associates found their way into exile in different parts of the globe, his poetry was almost wholly devoted to political objectives. The main aim at first was the promotion of a revolution which in fact never looked like getting off the ground, then after 1933 came the encouragement of resistance to Hitler. Brecht's output of that period not only includes a number of powerful satires which remain models of their kind, but also succeeds in developing certain intense political insights which had never before become matter for poetry. He was, as Walter Benjamin put it, the one living poet who 'asks himself where he ought to apply his talent, who applies it only where he is convinced of the need to do so, and who abstains on every other occasion'.

Though he continued to write on such themes, as the 30s moved on the principles laid down in 'Solely because of the increasing disorder' (p. 225) became less and less dominant in Brecht's work, and its centre of gravity shifted away from the day-to-day struggle. There was not only a still mystifying rift with Eisler which interrupted the political songs after 1935; there were also much more serious misgivings about Communist aesthetic policy and (with the launching of the great purges) Soviet justice. At the same time exile itself gave the poet the opportunity and also the stimulus to write a great deal more, presenting him with a whole range of new, politically-grounded private experience. In that great outpouring of Brecht's mature poetry, to which we owe the majority of the *Svendborg Poems*, he came to temper his directly political concerns – still evident in the 'German war primer' and 'German satires' of that collection – on the one hand with large-scale parables from antiquity and on the other with subtle, yet hard-headed observation of his own situation and surroundings. The Chinese influence in his work, filtering through the translations of Arthur Waley on which he based a series of 'Chinese poems', is henceforward often to be seen, leading to an increasing compression of the unrhymed verse and a new eye for the telling detail.

This spell of intense productivity lasted right through what Brecht called 'the dark times', in other words the steady march to war, the Stalinist purges and the Nazi victories of 1939–41. It continued in fact well past the publication of the *Svendborg Poems* till after he finally left Scandinavia for the United States. Then for a time the flow once more almost stopped. Two things seem at first to have had a paralysing effect on him there: Margarete Steffin's death on the journey through Russia, and the vain effort to adjust to the movie market where he hoped to get work. Though he did his best to overcome this, with the result that the American years do none the less occupy a distinctive place in his oeuvre, his poetry now settled at a rather more subdued level. The most striking thing here was the exile's-eye view of the Californian scene: his scepticism about its 'cheap prettiness' and refusal to forget the harsh desert just over the horizon, only waiting to come back. There was also the new domesticity of verses like 'Of sprinkling the garden' (p. 382), which surprised even the poet himself.

After that, in the immediate post-war years, there was at first a much more serious dearth of inspiration, with the Shelleyesque satire of 'The anachronistic procession' (p. 409) as the only poem of note before Brecht left America late in 1947. There was a rather faint renewal of interest once he had reached Germany a year later, followed by another small crop of poems in 1950 when the Berliner Ensemble had been set securely on its feet, and of course he was still enough of his old self to want to harness all his various talents to his country's reconstruction. None the less there is something a bit unconvincing about his more consciously committed poetry of that time, while the children's verses to which he now turned (as part of a general concern with young people) tend to ring false and artificial. Possibly Brecht saw these weaknesses himself, for another year of virtual silence followed before he began writing of more concrete, small-scale and immediate matters in the condensedly reflective vein of the 'Buckow Elegies', his last substantial sequence. From then to the end of his life the poetry was still rather thin in quantity but acutely observant of the East German scene, sometimes packing a sharp punch as in the belatedly published 'The solution' (p. 440) from the Buckow set. Torn between his loyalties and his doubts, he seems to have come to think twice about every utterance; but utter he

did. And once again he seems, however containedly, to have arrived at
the poetic style for what was most in his mind.

*   *   *

EDITORS' NOTE

For this paperback edition, the Brecht *Poems* have been split into three
parts. The first contains our selection up to 1928 (the year of *The Three-
penny Opera*); the second continues it up to 1938 (i.e. from the world
economic crisis to the eve of the war); while the third contains the re-
mainder, up to his death in 1956. Since the hardback volume from which
all three derive is comprised in the general English-language edition of
Brecht's work, those poems which occur elsewhere (i.e. primarily in the
plays) are excluded. A fourth, companion paperback will contain a
selection from them, and this will cover the whole time-span.

The pages of the present edition are numbered as in the hardback.
However, it excludes the critical apparatus of that large volume: i.e.
Brecht's own notes and comments on poetry, the note on 'The principal
collections of Brecht's poems' (relating the poems to his sometimes un-
realised plans for grouping and collecting them), and the fairly detailed
notes on separate poems, which also give particulars of musical settings.
The hardback volume also contains a much fuller introduction. Anybody
seeking this information will have to consult the hardback volume. The
paperbacks give the poems without explanation or comment.

The principles behind the selection, the general method of translation
and the decision not to print the German originals are explained in
the hardback introduction. The basic text followed is that of the 1967
German collected edition (major variations being shown in the notes).
However, unlike the original editors we have tried to follow a chrono-
logical arrangement. The aim is to show the development of Brecht's
poetry and its close relationship with the times through which he lived.

1 Early Poems and Psalms
1913–1920

THE BURNING TREE

Through the vaporous red fog of evening
We could see red flames like dizzy pillars
Smouldering shoot into the coal-black heaven.
In the fields below in sultry stillness
Crackling
There burned a tree.

High up stretched the rigid, panic-stricken branches
Black by dancing red surrounded
In a shower of sparks.
Through the fog great waves of fire flooded.
Dreadful the dry leaves all madly dancing
Jubilant, free, to end as ashes
Mockingly round the ancient trunk.

Yet, still and hugely lighting up the night
Like some historic warrior, tired, dead tired
But kingly yet in his despair
Stood the burning tree.

Then suddenly it raises high its blackened, rigid branches
Up leaps the purple flame towards its top –
Upright it stands awhile within the coal-black heaven

And then the trunk, surrounded by red sparks
Comes crashing.

SONG OF THE FORT DONALD RAILROAD GANG

1
The men of Fort Donald – wowee!
Made their way upstream where the forests forever soulless
        stand.
But one day the rain came down and the forests around them
        grew into a sea.

They were standing in water up to the knee.
   And morning's not going to come, they said
   And we'll all drown before dawn, they said
And dumbly they listened to the Erie wind.

2

The men of Fort Donald – wowee!
Stood by that water with their picks and rails and stared up
     at the darker sky
For it got dark, and evening rose out of the rippling sea.
No, not a scrap of sky showed hopefully.
   And we are tired now, they said
   And we may fall asleep, they said
And no sun will wake us by and by.

3

The men of Fort Donald – wowee!
Further said: if we go to sleep, it's goodbye . . .
For out of water and night sleep grew, and they were a herd,
     fidgety.
One said: sing 'Johnny Over the Sea'.
   Yes, that might keep us awake, they said
   Yes, we'll sing his song, they said
And they sang about Johnny over the sea.

4

The men of Fort Donald – wowee!
Blind as moles they went groping in that dark Ohio ground
But they sang loud, as if some good thing was on the way
Yes, they'd never made such a sound.
   Oh where is my Johnny tonight, they sang
   Oh where is my Johnny tonight, they sang
And under them Ohio grew wet, and the rain and wind
     around.

5

The men of Fort Donald – wowee!
Will stay awake now and sing until they are drowned.

But by dawn the water is higher than they, and louder than
        they the Erie winds cry.
    Where is my Johnny tonight, they sing
    This Ohio is wet, they say
Water is all that's awake that morning, and the Erie wind.

6
The men of Fort Donald – wowee!
The trains scream rushing over them alongside Lake Erie
And the wind at that spot sings a stupid melody
And the pine forest screams after the train: wowee!
    That time morning never came, they scream
    They were drowned before dawn, they scream
These evenings our wind often sings their 'Johnny Over the
        Sea'.

THE LEGEND OF THE HARLOT EVELYN ROE

When springtime came and the sea was blue
(Her heart kept beating so)
There came on board with the last boat
A girl called Evelyn Roe.

She wore a hair shirt next her skin
Which was unearthly fair.
She wore no gold or ornament
Except her wondrous hair.

'Oh Captain, take me with you to the Holy Land
I must go to Jesus Christ.'
'We'll take you because we are fools and you are
Of women the loveliest.'

'May He reward you. I'm only a poor girl.
My soul belongs to Christ our Lord.'
'Then give your sweet body to us, my dear

The Lord you love cannot pay for you
Because He is long since dead.'

They sailed along in sun and wind
And they loved Evelyn Roe.
She ate their bread and drank their wine
And wept as she did so.

They danced by night. They danced by day
They left the helm alone.
Evelyn Roe was so sweet and so soft:
They were harder than stone.

The springtime went. The summer passed.
At night she ran in worn-out shoes
In the grey light from mast to mast
And looked for a peaceful shore
Poor girl, poor Evelyn Roe.

She danced at night. She danced by day
And she was sick and tired.
'Oh, Captain, when shall we get there
To the city of Our Lord?'

The captain was lying in her lap
And kissed her and laughed too.
'If someone's to blame if we never get there
That someone is Evelyn Roe.'

She danced at night. She danced by day.
And she was deathly tired.
They were sick of her from the captain down
To the youngest boy on board.

She wore a silk dress next her skin
Which was rough with scabs and sores
And round her blemished forehead hung
A filthy tangle of hair.

'I shall never see you, Christ my Lord
My flesh is too sinful for you.
You cannot come to a common whore
And I am a bad woman now.'

She ran for hours from mast to mast
And her heart and her feet were sore
Till one dark night when no one watched
She went to find that shore.

That was in chilly January
She swam a long way in cold seas
And it isn't till March or even April
That the buds come out on the trees.

She gave herself to the dark waves, and they
Washed her white and fair
Now she will reach the Holy Land
Before the captain is there.

In spring when she came to Heaven's gates
Saint Peter slammed them to.
'God has told me he will not have
The harlot Evelyn Roe.'

But when she came to the gates of Hell
She found they'd bolted them to.
The Devil shouted 'I will not have
The pious Evelyn Roe.'

So she wandered through wind and through starry space
Not knowing where to go.
Late one evening I saw her crossing a field:
She stumbled often. She never stood still.
Poor girl, poor Evelyn Roe.

MODEL OF A NASTY FELLOW

1

By the boneyard, lulled by Lethe
Scarred by frost and blue as slate
From between his blackened teeth he
Let cold laughter emanate.
Yes, he spewed it at the altar
Like a yellow gob of spit
By dead cats and fish-heads caught there:
And the sun shone cool on it.

2

Only . . .

3

Where'll he turn when fall the shadows
Whom a mother's curse repays –
Who has slain the lambs of widows
Drunk the milk of waifs and strays?
Will the Good Shepherd perceive him
Belching, full of fatted calf?
Is Our Lady to receive him
Hung with virgins' scalps, and laugh?

4

Pushing hair down from his forehead
Seaweed-like across his face
Does he hope to hide his horrid
Clinkered insolent grimace?
Watch his nasty naked features
Twitching: is that to persuade
God to save one of His creatures
Or because he is afraid?

5

At the end, on his death bed, he
Did a quick shit in the sheet –

Surely, though, they'll know already
What he'd had down here to eat?
Throughout life he always drew the
Dirtiest and shortest straw.
Is he now supposed to do the
Grateful thing, and ask for more?

Therefore now I beg you, have compassion
On such swine, and on their pigswill even!
Pray with me that God grants them admission
To the treasures of His heaven!

HYMN TO GOD

1

Deep in the darkest valleys the hungry are perishing.
You merely show them bread and leave them to perish.
You merely lord it eternal, invisible
Beaming and brutal over the infinite plan.

2

You let the young men die and those who enjoy their life
But those who wanted to die you would not accept . . .
Many of those who now lie rotting away
Had faith in you, and died completely secure.

3

You let the poor stay poor for year after year
Feeling that their desires were sweeter than your paradise
Too bad they died before you had brought them the light
But they died in bliss all the same – and rotted at once.

4

Many of us say you are not – and a good thing too.
But how could *that* thing not be which can play such a trick?
If so much lives by you and could not die without you –
Tell me how far does it matter that you don't exist?

THE HEAVEN FOR DISENCHANTED MEN

1

Half-way along the road from night to morning
Naked and frozen in a rock-strewn glen
A chilly sky across it like an awning
You'll find the heaven for disenchanted men.

2

Every thousand years white clouds will hover
Up in the heavens. A thousand years go by
With none. But every thousand years there are some
Up in the heavens. White and smiling. High.

3

Ever silence where great rocks are lying
The glow remains although the light has gone
Sullen souls, fed up with their own crying
Sit dreamless, dumb and very much alone.

4

Yet from lower heavens there'll be singing
At times, in voices dignified and true:
You'll hear at times the gentle hymns go winging
From the adorers' heaven, and some get through.

FAIRGROUND SONG

Spring leapt through sky's hoop
On to the grassy plain
With barrel organ and with pipe
The gaudy fair was here again.

A child that I saw there
Has hair of shining gold
And eyes that become her
A wonder to behold.

And every roundabout
Is turning in the sun –
And when they come to rest
My head whirls on.

The roundabouts are still at night
Like globes of frosted glass
Every night is starry bright
Let's see what comes to pass!

I'm drunk now, my dear
And all will deride
This Chinese lantern here
I've got for a head.

Now let the spring proceed
I'll see it evermore:
I have seen a child
And she has golden hair.

ABOUT A PAINTER

Neher Cas rides across the sands of the desert on a dromedary
    and paints a green date palm in water-colours
(under heavy machine-gun fire).

It's war. The terrible sky is bluer than usual.

Many fall dead in the marsh-grass.
You can shoot brown men dead. In the evening you can paint
    them. They often have remarkable hands.

Neher Cas paints the pale sky above the Ganges in the
    morning wind.
Seven coolies prop up his canvas; fourteen coolies prop up
    Neher Cas, who has been drinking
because the sky is beautiful.

Neher Cas sleeps on the stones at night and curses because
   they are hard.
But that too he finds beautiful (the cursing included)
He would like to paint it.

Neher Cas paints the violet sky above Peshawar white because
   he's got no blue left in the tube.
Slowly the sun eats him up. His soul is transfigured.
Neher Cas painteth for evermore.

At sea between Ceylon and Port Said, on the inside of the old
   sailing ship's hull, he paints
his best picture, using three colours and the light from two
   portholes.
Then the ship sank, he got away. Cas is proud of the picture.
It was not for sale.

ORGE'S LIST OF WISHES

Of joys, the unweighed.
Of skins, the unflayed.

Of stories, the incomprehensible.
Of suggestions, the indispensable.

Of girls, the new.
Of women, the untrue.

Of orgasms, the uncoordinated.
Of enmities, the reciprocated.

Of abodes, the impermanent.
Of partings, the unexuberant.

Of arts, the unexploitable.
Of teachers, the forgettable.

Of pleasures, the unsurreptitious.
Of aims, the adventitious.

Of enemies, the delicate.
Of friends, the unsophisticate.

Of greens, the emerald.
Of messages, the herald.

Of the elements, fire.
Of the gods, the higher.

Of the stricken, the deferential.
Of the seasons, the torrential.

Of lives, the lucid.
Of deaths, the rapid.

ORGE'S REPLY ON BEING
SENT A SOAPED NOOSE

1
He told us how nice it would be
If his life took a better course:
His life was as bad as it could be –
But he himself was worse.

2
The soap and the noose he accepted
For he said it was a shame
Living on this planet
How dirty one became.

3
And yet there were mountains and valleys
On which one had never set eye:

So it paid to restrict one's sallies
To selectively – passing by.

4

As long as the sun was our neighbour
There must be some hope yet:
He'd wait as long as it stayed there
And as long as it knew how to set.

5

There were plenty of beeches and larches
All very conveniently made
For hanging oneself from their branches
Or stretching oneself in their shade.

6

All the same, there's a final possession
Which a man won't give up with good grace
Yes, it's his final excretion
On which he'll be resting his case.

7

Once the hatred and venom he'd swallowed
Rose to more than his gullet could take
He would just draw a knife from his pocket
And languidly slit through his neck.

LITTLE SONG

1

One time there was a man
Whose drinking bouts began
When he was eighteen . . . So
That was what laid him low.
He died in his eightieth year:
What of, is crystal clear.

2
One time there was a child
Which died when one year old
Quite prematurely . . . So
That was what laid it low.
It never drank, that's clear
And died aged just one year.

3
Which helps you to assess
Alcohol's harmlessness.

THE SONG OF THE CLOUD OF THE NIGHT

My heart is dull as the cloud of the night
And homeless, oh my dear!
The cloud in the sky over trees and land
Who do not know what for.
The distance stretches all around.

My heart is wild as the cloud of the night
And aching, oh my dear!
Which would be the whole wide sky on its own
And does not know what for.
The cloud of the night and the wind are alone.

UTTERANCES OF A MARTYR

I, for instance, play billiards in the attic
Where they hang the washing up to dry and let it piss.
Day after day my mother says: It's tragic
For a grown-up person to be like this.

And to say such things, when no normal person would look
    at things that way.

Among the washing too . . . I call it unhealthy, sheer
    pornography.
But how fed up I get with having to watch everything I say
And I tell my mother: That's what washing's like, why blame
    me?

Then she says: You ought to rinse out your mouth; it's a
    sewer.
Then I say: I don't put it in my mouth, you know
And: To the pure all things are pure
After all, it's quite natural to make water, I've even known
    dogs to do so.

Then, naturally, she cries and says: But the washing! And
    that I'd soon have her under the sod at this rate
And the day would come when I'd want to claw it up to get
    her back once more
But it would be too late by then, and I'd start finding out
How much she'd done for me. But I should have thought of
    that before.

The only answer then is to go off and choke down your
    scepticism
At the use of such weapons, and smoke till you've recharged
    your batteries.
What business have they got putting that stuff about Truth
    in the catechism
If one's not allowed to say what is?

OF FRANÇOIS VILLON

1
François Villon was a poor man's son
The cool breeze sang his only lullaby.

All through his youth in sleet and wind the one
Thing beautiful around was endless sky.
François Villon, who never had a bed to lie in
Found soon enough cool wind was satisfying.

2

With bruised backside and bleeding feet, he found
Stones are keener than rock to lacerate.
He soon learned to cast stones at those around
And, once he'd skinned them all, to celebrate.
   And if it stretched to something fortifying
   He soon enough found stretching satisfying.

3

God's table was denied to him for life
So Heaven's blessed gifts he could not get.
His fate it was to stab men with his knife
And stick his neck into the traps they set.
   So let them kiss his arse while he was trying
   To eat some food that he found satisfying.

4

He got no glimpse of Heaven's sweet rewards
Policemen broke his pride with their big hands
Yet he too was a child of our dear Lord's –
Long time he rode through wind and rain towards
Where his only reward, the gibbet, stands.

5

François Villon was never caught, but died
Concealed among some bushes, dodging gaol –
His ribald soul however will abide
Deathless as this my song which cannot stale.
   And when he lay, poor wretch, stretched out there dying
   He found this stretching too was satisfying.

BALLAD OF THE PIRATES

1

Frantic with brandy from their plunder
Drenched in the blackness of the gale
Splintered by frost and stunned by thunder
Hemmed in the crows-nest, ghostly pale
Scorched by the sun through tattered shirt
(The winter sun kept them alive)
Amid starvation, sickness, dirt
So sang the remnant that survived:
   Oh heavenly sky of streaming blue!
   Enormous wind, the sails blow free!
   Let wind and heavens go hang! But oh
   Sweet Mary, let us keep the sea!

2

No waving fields with gentle breezes
Or dockside bar with raucous band
No dance hall warm with gin and kisses
No gambling hell kept them on land.
They very quickly tired of fighting
By midnight girls began to pall:
Their rotten hulk seemed more inviting
That ship without a flag at all.
   Oh heavenly sky of streaming blue!
   Enormous wind, the sails blow free!
   Let wind and heavens go hang! But oh
   Sweet Mary, let us keep the sea!

3

Riddled with rats, its bilges oozing
With pestilence and puke and piss
They swear by her when they're out boozing
And cherish her just as she is.
In storms they'll reckon their position
Lashed to the halyards by their hair:

They'd go to heaven on one condition –
That she can find a mooring there.
   Oh heavenly sky of streaming blue!
   Enormous wind, the sails blow free!
   Let wind and heavens go hang! But oh
   Sweet Mary, let us keep the sea!

4

They loot their wine and belch with pleasure
While bales of silk and bars of gold
And precious stones and other treasure
Weigh down the rat-infested hold.
To grace their limbs, all hard and shrunken
Sacked junks yield vari-coloured stuffs
Till out their knives come in some drunken
Quarrel about a pair of cuffs.
   Oh heavenly sky of streaming blue!
   Enormous wind, the sails blow free!
   Let wind and heavens go hang! But oh
   Sweet Mary, let us keep the sea!

5

They murder coldly and detachedly
Whatever comes across their path
They throttle gullets as relaxedly
As fling a rope up to the mast.
At wakes they fall upon the liquor
Then stagger overboard and drown
While the remainder give a snigger
And wave a toe as they go down.
   Oh heavenly sky of streaming blue!
   Enormous wind, the sails blow free!
   Let wind and heavens go hang! But oh
   Sweet Mary, let us keep the sea!

6

Across a violet horizon
Caught in the ice by pale moonlight

On pitch-black nights when mist is rising
And half the ship is lost from sight
They lurk like wolves between the hatches
And murder for the fun of it
And sing to keep warm in their watches
Like children drumming as they shit.
 Oh heavenly sky of streaming blue!
 Enormous wind, the sails blow free!
 Let wind and heavens go hang! But oh
 Sweet Mary, let us keep the sea!

7

They take their hairy bellies with them
To stuff with food on foreign ships
Then stretch them out in sweet oblivion
Athwart the foreign women's hips.
In gentle winds, in blue unbounded
Like noble beasts they graze and play
And often seven bulls have mounted
Some foreign girl they've made their prey.
 Oh heavenly sky of streaming blue!
 Enormous wind, the sails blow free!
 Let wind and heavens go hang! But oh
 Sweet Mary, let us keep the sea!

8

Once you have danced till you're exhausted
And boozed until your belly sags
Though sun and moon unite their forces –
Your appetite for fighting flags.
Brilliant with stars, the night will shake them
While music plays, in gentle ease
And wind will fill their sails and take them
To other, undiscovered seas.
 Oh heavenly sky of streaming blue!
 Enormous wind, the sails blow free!

Let wind and heavens go hang! But oh
Sweet Mary, let us keep the sea!

9

But then upon an April evening
Without a star by which to steer
The placid ocean, softly heaving
Decides that they must disappear.
The boundless sky they love is hiding
The stars in smoke that shrouds their sight
While their beloved winds are sliding
The clouds towards the gentle light.
  Oh heavenly sky of streaming blue!
  Enormous wind, the sails blow free!
  Let wind and heavens go hang! But oh
  Sweet Mary, let us keep the sea!

10

At first they're fanned by playful breezes
Into the night they mustn't miss
The velvet sky smiles once, then closes
Its hatches on the black abyss.
Once more they feel the kindly ocean
Watching beside them on their way
The wind then lulls them with its motion
And kills them all by break of day.
  Oh heavenly sky of streaming blue!
  Enormous wind, the sails blow free!
  Let wind and heavens go hang! But oh
  Sweet Mary, let us keep the sea!

11

Once more the final wave is tossing
The cursed vessel to the sky
When suddenly it clears, disclosing
The mighty reef on which they lie.
And, at the last, a strange impression

While rigging screams and storm winds howl
Of voices hurtling to perdition
Yet once more singing, louder still:
   Oh heavenly sky of streaming blue!
   Enormous wind, the sails blow free!
   Let wind and heavens go hang! But oh
   Sweet Mary, let us keep the sea!

SONG OF THE SOLDIER OF THE RED ARMY

1

Because our land is eaten up
With an exhausted sun in it
It spat us out on to dark pavements
And country roads of frozen grit.

2

The melting slush washed the army in the spring
It was a child of summer's red.
Then in October snow began to fall
In January's winds its breast froze dead.

3

In those years talk of Freedom came
From lips inside which ice had cracked
And you saw many with jaws like tigers
Following the red, inhuman flag.

4

And when the moon swam red across the fields
Each resting on his horse's side
They often spoke about the times that were coming
Then fell asleep, made sluggish by the ride.

5

In rain and in the murky wind
Hard stone seemed good to sleep upon.

The rain washed out our filthy eyes and cleansed them
Of filth and many a varied sin.

6
Often at night the sky turned red
They thought red dawn had come again.
That was a fire, but the dawn came also.
Freedom, my children, never came.

7
And so, wherever they might be
They looked around and said, it's hell.
The time went by. The latest hell, though
Was never the very last hell of all.

8
So many hells were still to come.
Freedom, my children, never came.
The time goes by. But if the heavens came now
Those heavens would be much the same.

9
When once our body's eaten up
With an exhausted heart in it
The army spews our skin and bones out
Into cold and shallow pits.

10
And with our body hard from rain
And with our heart all scarred by ice
And with our bloodstained empty hands we
Come grinning into your paradise.

APFELBÖCK, OR THE LILY OF THE FIELD

1

Mild was the light as Jakob Apfelböck
Struck both his father and his mother down
And shut their bodies in the linen press
And hung about the house all on his own.

2

The clouds went floating past beneath the sky
Around his house the summer winds blew mild
Inside the house he passed the time away
Who just a week before was still a child.

3

The days went by, the nights went by as well
And nothing changed except a thing or two.
Beside his parents Jakob Apfelböck
Waited to see what time would find to do.

4

The woman still delivers milk each day
Sweet thick cool skim milk, left behind the door.
What Jakob doesn't drink he pours away
For Jakob's hardly drinking any more.

5

The paper man still brings the paper round
He steps up to the house with heavy tread
And stuffs the paper in the letter box
But Jakob Apfelböck leaves it unread.

6

And when the smell of corpses filled the house
Jakob felt queasy and began to cry.
Tearfully, Jakob Apfelböck moved out
And slept henceforward on the balcony.

7

Up spoke the paper man then on his round:
What is that smell? Something gone off, I'd say.
The light was mild as Jakob Apfelböck
Said: Just some dirty clothes I shut away.

8

Up spoke the milk woman then on her round:
What is that smell? I'd say that something's died.
The light was mild as Jakob Apfelböck
Said: Just some meat that mother put aside.

9

And when they came to open the press door
Jakob stood by, the light was mild and clear
And when they asked him what he did it for
Said Jakob Apfelböck: I've no idea.

10

A few days later the milk woman said
She wondered what would happen by and by:
Would Jakob Apfelböck, the child, perhaps
Visit the grave where his poor parents lie?

THE SHIP

1

Through the clear seas of countless oceans swimming
With sharks as escorts under red moons skimming
I tossed and shed direction, cast off gravity.
My timbers rotting and my sails in tatters
My ropes decaying in the salty waters
My horizon grew remoter, paler too my sky.

2

Since it turned paler and the remote horizon
Left me abandoned in my watery prison

I knew I must go down, and understood.
Once I had realised that there's no resistance
These seas must put an end to my existence
I let the waters take me where they would.

3

And the waters came, and swept vast numbers
Of creatures through me, so that in my timbers
Creature befriended creature in the gloom.
Once the sky fell through the rotting hatches
And they knew each other in the watches
And the sharks inside me felt at home.

4

Three moons passed, I filled with floating seaweeds
Which clutched my wood and greened across my bulkheads
Until my face told yet another tale.
Green and groaning deep below my middle
Slowly I moved, suffering but little
Weighed down by weed and moon, by shark and whale.

5

To gulls and seaweed I was a kind of haven
Not to be blamed because I failed to save them.
How slow and full I shall be as I drown
Now, eight moons gone, the waters spurting quickly
Through all my flanks, my face grows yet more sickly.
And I pray that I may soon go down.

6

Unknown fishermen saw something nearing
Which as it neared seemed to be disappearing.
Was it an island? Or a raft passed by?
Something moved, agleam with seagulls' spatter
Loaded with moon and corpses, weed and water
Silent and stout towards the washed-out sky.

OF CORTEZ'S MEN

On the seventh day, when the winds were gentle
The meadows grew brighter. As the sun was good
They thought of resting. Rolled out brandy
From the waggons and unhitched some oxen.
They slaughtered them that evening. As it grew cooler
They hacked from timber in the marsh near by
Arm-thick branches, knotty, good for burning.
Then they set to devouring highly spiced meat
And about the ninth hour, singing
Began to drink. The night was cool and green.
Throats hoarsened, soundly soused and sated
With a last cool look at the big stars
They went to sleep by the fire towards midnight.
They slept deep, but many a one in the morning
Knew he'd heard the oxen bellow – once.
Waking at noon, they're already in the forest.
Glazed eyes, dull limbs, groaning
They hobble up and see in wonder
Arm-thick branches, knotty, all round them
Higher than a man, much tangled with foliage
And small sweet-smelling flowers.
It grows sultry under their roof; this
Seems to be thickening. The hot sun
Is not to be seen nor the sky either.
The captain bellows like a bull for axes
But they're over there where the oxen are lowing.
Out of sight. Foully cursing, they stumble
About the camp, knocking against the branches
That have crept between them.
Arms slack, they hurl themselves wildly
Into the growth, which slightly shivers
As though stirred by a light breeze from outside it.
After hours of work gloomily they press their sweating
Foreheads against the alien branches.
The branches grew and the horrible tangle

Slowly grew over them. Later, at evening
Which was darker because of the foliage growing
They sat silent with fear, like apes in
Their cages, dead beat with hunger.
The tangle of branches grew that night. But there was
         probably moonlight
For it was still quite light; they could still see each other.
Only towards morning the stuff was so dense that
They never saw each other again before they died.
The next day a singing rose from the forest
Muffled and waning. Probably they sang to each other.
That night it grew stiller. The oxen too were silent.
Towards morning it was as if beasts bellowed
But fairly far off. Later came hours
When all was quiet. The forest slowly
In the gentle wind and the good sun, quietly
Ate up the meadows in the weeks that came.

OF THE FRIENDLINESS OF THE WORLD

1

To this windy world of chill distress
You all came in utter nakedness
Cold you lay and destitute of all
Till a woman wrapped you in a shawl.

2

No one called you, none bade you approach
And you were not fetched by groom and coach.
Strangers were you in this early land
When a man once took you by the hand.

3

From this windy world of chill distress
You all part in rot and filthiness.
Almost everyone has loved the world
When on him two clods of earth are hurled.

OF CLIMBING IN TREES

1

When you come up at evening from your waters
(For you must all be naked, and with tender skin)
Climb then in your great trees still higher
In the light wind. The sky too should be wan.
Seek out great trees that in the evening
Slowly and sombrely rock their topmost boughs.
And wait among their foliage for darkness
With bat and nightmare close about your brows.

2

The little stiff leaves of the undergrowth
Are sure to graze your backs, which you must squeeze
Firmly between the branches; thus you'll climb
Groaning a little, higher in the trees.
It is quite fine to rock upon the tree.
But rocking with the knees one can't permit
You should be to the tree as his own top has been:
A hundred years of evenings: he rocks it.

OF SWIMMING IN LAKES AND RIVERS

1

In the pale summer when the winds above
Only in great trees' leaves a murmur make
You ought to lie in rivers or in ponds
As do the waterweeds which harbour pike.
The body grows light in the water. When your arm
Falls easily from water into sky
The little wind rocks it absentmindedly
Taking it likely for a brownish bough.

2

The sky at noon offers ample calm.
You close your eyes when swallows pass.

The mud is warm. Cool bubbles welling up
Show that a fish has just swum through us.
My body and thighs and resting arm
We lie in the water quite at one and still
Only when the cool fish swim through us
I sense the sun shining above the pool.

3

By the evening having grown very lazy
With lying so long, each limb begins to smart
You have to dash all that with a reckless smack
Into blue streams which scatter far apart.
It's best to last out until the evening
For then the pale shark-like sky will come
Evil and greedy over bush and river
And all things will assume their aptest form.

4

Of course you must lie upon your back
As if by habit. And drift along.
You need not swim, no, only behave as if
It's just to the mass of gravel you belong.
You should look at the sky and act
As if a woman held you, which is right.
Quite without great upheaval as the good God does
When he swims in his rivers at evening light.

BALLAD OF THE DEATH OF ANNA CLOUDFACE

1

Seven years went by. With gin and with whisky
He swilled her face right out of his brain
And the hole in the air grew blacker, and full of
The flood of liquor this brain became bare.

2

With gin and tobacco, with organs and orgies:
What was her face like, when she vanished from here?
What was her face like? Did it merge in the cloud-drifts?
Hey, there, face! This white page met his stare.

3

Wherever he travelled, on how many shores
(He didn't just go there as you would or I)
A voice cried out to him white on the waters
A voice from lips that were fading away . . .

4

Once more he sees her face: in the cloud drift.
Very pale by now. Since he lingered too long . . .
Once more in the wind he heard her voice, faintly
Far off in the wind which was driving the cloud . . .

5

But in later years he had nothing
Left but the cloud and wind, and they
Began to be silent as she was
And like her to fade away.

6

Oh, when soaked with the salt of the waters
His wild hands gashed raw by the lash of wild gales
He drifts down, the last thing he hears is
A sea mew still crying above the sails.

7

Of those green bitternesses, of the winds and
The skies flying by, of the snowfields that shine
And whisky, tobacco and organs there's nothing
Left but a scream in the air, a mouthful of brine.

8

But always up to those hills that are wilting
Away high above in wild April's winds white
Like cloud-drifts fly his desires ever paling:
A face goes by. And a mouth falls mute.

ANNA SPEAKS ILL OF BIDI

Bursting with conceit none matches
Lazy as a giant sloth
All he does, sits there and scratches
At his balls while he holds forth.

Smokes cigars and reads the papers
Swigs schnapps, haunts the billiard hall
Ice-cold, with his airs and capers
No humanity at all.

All week banging every whore
Far too lazy for a piss.
He grins, you see stumps, no more
Not a whole tooth in his face.

But a providence above'll
Stop him having the last laugh
Someone's going to take a shovel
Smartly slice his head in half.

Yes, he'll crawl before he's finished
Sooner or later he'll get his.
If they let him go unpunished
What's the point of Nemesis?

'FALADA, FALADA, THERE THOU ART HANGING!'

I hauled my cart, though I felt weak
I got as far as Frankfurt Street
There I start thinking: Oh, Oh
How weak I feel. Perhaps
If I let go
I'll collapse.
Ten minutes later just my bones were on the street.

For I'd hardly fallen flat
(The driver rushed to the telephone)
When up the street
Ran hungry people, pitterpat, pitterpat
To get their pound of meat.
They hacked my flesh from the bone
And me still alive! Hadn't yet done with dying.

These people, I'd known them before!
Draped me with sacks, they did, to keep the flies away
Gave me bits of old bread
And more –
To the driver, *You be nice and kind*, they'd said.
Such friends once; such enemies today.
They were suddenly different; what on earth had happened?

Then I asked myself: this coldness, why? Now what
In all the world can have come over them?
Who's bugging this lot
To make them act
As if they're cold right through?
Help them. Be quick, too.
Or a thing you thought never could might happen to you.

REPORT ON A TICK

The book that he has written
Makes me yawn.
There are seven times seven
Commandments therein.

1

Through our dreams of childhood
In the bed of milky white
Round apple trees there haunted
The man in violet.

2

Lying in the dust near him
We watched how he sat. Idly
And stroked his pigeon
And basked by the pathway.

3

He swigs blood like a tick
Cherishes the smallest gift
And all that is yours he'll take
So that he's all you have left.

4

And you who gave up for him
Your joy and others' too
And lie, a beggar, on the ground
He will not know you.

5

To spit right in your face
Is splendid fun, he'd think
And he will lie in wait
To catch you on the blink.

6

After dark he'll stand and pry
Over your windowsill
And go off huffily
Remembering every smile.

7

And if you feel joyful
And laugh however low
Upon his little organ
A mournful tune he'll play.

8

If someone mocks at him
He'll plunge in heaven's blue
And yet he made the sows
In his own image too.

9

Of all bedsides he loves
Most by deathbeds to sit.
He haunts our last fevers
That man in violet.

REMEMBERING MARIE A.

It was a day in that blue month September
Silent beneath a plum tree's slender shade
I held her there, my love so pale and silent
As if she were a dream that must not fade.
Above us in the shining summer heaven
There was a cloud my eyes dwelt long upon
It was quite white and very high above us
Then I looked up, and found that it had gone.

And since that day so many moons, in silence
Have swum across the sky and gone below.

The plum trees surely have been chopped for firewood
And if you ask, how does that love seem now?
I must admit: I really can't remember
And yet I know what you are trying to say.
But what her face was like I know no longer
I only know: I kissed it on that day.

As for the kiss, I'd long ago forgot it
But for the cloud that floated in the sky
I know that still, and shall for ever know it
It was quite white and moved in very high.
It may be that the plum trees still are blooming
That woman's seventh child may now be there
And yet that cloud had only bloomed for minutes
When I looked up, it vanished on the air.

Thirteen Psalms

PSALM IN SPRINGTIME

1 Now I'm on the lookout for summer, lads.

2 We've bought rum and have put new strings on the guitar. White shirts have still to be acquired.

3 Our limbs grow like the grass in June and in mid-August the virgins disappear. It's the time of boundless rapture.

4 Day after day the sky fills with a gentle radiance and its nights take your sleep away.

GOD'S EVENING SONG

When the misty blue wind of evening wakes God the Father he sees the sky above him turn pale and he enjoys it. Then the great cosmic chorale refreshes his ears and sends him into transports:

The cry of flooded forests which are on the point of drowning.

The groaning of old, brown frame houses under too great a weight of furniture and people.

The hacking cough of exhausted fields, robbed of their vigour.

The gigantic abdominal rumbling that marked the end of the last mammoth's hard and blissful life on earth.

The anxious prayers of the mothers of great men.

The roaring glaciers of the white Himalaya, disporting in icy isolation.

And the anguish of Bert Brecht, who is not doing too well.

And simultaneously: the mad songs of the waters rising in the forests.

The gentle breathing of sleeping people, rocked by old floorboards.

The ecstatic murmuring of cornfields, grinding out endless prayers.

The great talk of great men.

And the wonderful songs of Bert Brecht, who is not doing too well..

VISION IN WHITE

1 At night I am woken up, bathed in sweat, by a cough which strangles me. My room is too small. It is full of archangels.

2 I know I have loved too much. I have stuffed too many bodies, used up too many orange skies. I ought to be stamped out.

3 The white bodies, the softest of them, have stolen my warmth, they went away from me fat. Now I'm freezing. Many blankets are piled on top of me, I'm suffocating.

4 I suspect they will want to fumigate me with incense. My room is flooded with holy water. They say: I have got holy water dropsy. And that's fatal.

5 My sweethearts bring a bit of quicklime with them, in hands which I have kissed. The bill comes for the orange skies, the bodies and the rest. I cannot pay it.

6 Better to die. – I lean back. I close my eyes. The archangels applaud.

FREIGHT

1 I have heard that lovemaking can give you a swollen throat. I don't want one. But the swing-boats, I have heard, can give you a swollen throat too. So I shan't be able to avoid it.

2 The red tarpaulins, in which one wraps oneself and the boats as well when flying, clap their applause, the stanchions of big boats grind their teeth, because they've got to go up, I compare them to animals gnashing at the bit, but their rider is sitting tight. He has a grip like a tick, bloodthirsty; the horrible polyp, he hugs the fat crimson beast and rides skyward, where sails catch him. The yellow lamps look up goggling to see how high we can go without making the whole machine explode.

SWING-BOATS

1 One has to push one's knees forward like a royal whore, as if supported by knees. Very big. And crimson death-plunges into the naked sky, and one flies forward, one moment arse-first, and obverse face forward the next. We are stark naked, the wind fumbles through our clothes. We were born like that.

2 The music never stops. Angels blow panpipes in a round dance so that it almost bursts. One soars into the sky, one soars over the earth, sister air, sister! Brother wind! Time passes but the music never.

3 Eleven o'clock at night and the swings close down, so that the Good Lord can carry on swinging.

SONG ABOUT A SWEETHEART

1 I know it, sweethearts: because of my wild life I'm losing my hair, and I have to sleep on the stones. You see me drinking the cheapest gin, and I walk naked in the wind.

2 But there was a time, sweethearts, when I was pure.

3 I had a woman; she was stronger than me, as the grass is stronger than the bull: it stands up again.

4 She saw that I was wicked, and she loved me.

5 She did not ask where the path led, which was her path, and perhaps it led downhill. When she gave me her body she said: that is all. And her body became my body.

6 Now she's nowhere, she vanished like a cloud after rain, I let her go and she went downwards, for that was her path.

7 But at night, sometimes, when you see me drinking, I see her face, pale in the wind, strong and turned towards me, and I bow to her in the wind.

SONG ABOUT MY MOTHER

1 I no longer remember her face as it was before her pains began. Wearily, she pushed the black hair back from her forehead, which was bony, I can still see her hand as she does it.

2 Twenty winters had threatened her, her sufferings were legion, death was ashamed to approach her. Then she died, and they discovered that her body was like a child's.

3 She grew up in the forest.

4 She died among faces which had looked so long at her dying that they had grown hard. One forgave her for suffering, but she was wandering among those faces before she collapsed.

5 There are many who leave us without our detaining them. We have said all there is to say, there is nothing more between them and us, our faces hardened as we parted. But we did not say the important things, but saved on essentials.

6 Oh why do we not say the important things, it would be so easy, and we are damned because we do not. Easy words, they were, pressing against our teeth; they fell out as we laughed, and now they choke us.

7 Now my mother has died, yesterday towards evening, on the First of May. One won't be able to claw her up out again with one's fingernails.

OF HE

1 Listen, friends, I'll sing you the song of He, the dark-skinned girl, my sweetheart for the sixteen months before she fell apart.

2 She didn't grow old, she had undiscriminating hands, she sold her skin for a cup of tea and her self for a whip. She ran among the willows till she was tired out, He did.

3 She offered herself like a fruit, but nobody accepted her. Many had her in their mouths and spat her out again, the good He. He, the sweetheart.

4 She knew in her brain what a woman is, but not in her knees, by day she knew the way with her eyes, but in the dark she did not.

5 At night she was miserable, blind with vanity, He, and women are night animals, and she was no night animal.

6 She wasn't wise like Bie, the graceful, Bie the plant, she just kept on running around and her heart was without thought.

7 Therefore she died in the fifth month of the year 1920, a quick death, secretly, when nobody was watching, and she went away like a cloud of which it is said that it never was.

10TH PSALM

1 Quite definitely: I'm crazy. I won't last much longer. I just had time to go crazy.

2 Whenever I go under, women still stand around, white ones, with raised arms, their palms pressed together.

3 I drug myself with music, the bitter absinthe of small town bands, organs of the electric kind, they left their dregs in me, I know. But it is my last distraction.

4 I read the last letters of great men and from the brown imitation Arabs before the canvas booths I steal their most effective gestures. I'm only doing all this for the time being.

SONG ABOUT THE WOMAN

1 Evenings by the river in the dark heart of the bushes I see her face again sometimes, face of the woman I loved: my woman, who is dead now.

2 It was many years ago and at times I no longer know anything about her, once she was everything, but everything passes.

3 And she was in me like a little juniper on the Mongolian steppes, concave, with a pale yellow sky and great sadness.

4 We lived in a black hut beside the river. The horseflies often stung her white body and I read the paper seven times or I said: your hair is the colour of dirt. Or: you have no heart.

5 But one day as I was washing my shirt in the hut she went to the door and looked at me, wanting to go away.

6 And he who had beaten her till he was tired said: my angel –

7 And he who had said: I love you – took her out and looked at the sky, smiling, and praised the weather and shook her hand.

8 Now that she was outside in the open air and the hut grew desolate he shut the door and sat down behind the paper.

9 Since then I haven't seen her, and all that remained of her was the little cry she gave when she came back to the door in the morning and found it shut.

10 Now my hut has rotted away and my breast is stuffed with newspaper and I lie by the river, evenings, in the dark heart of the bushes and I remember.

11 The wind has the smell of grass in its hair, and the water cries endlessly to God for peace, and on my tongue there is a bitter taste.

THE FIRST PSALM

1 How terrifying it is in the night, the convex face of the black land!

2 Above the world are the clouds, they belong to the world. Above the clouds there is nothing.

3 The solitary tree in the stony field must be feeling it is all in vain. It has never seen a tree. There are no trees.

4 I keep on thinking we are not observed. The leprosy of the sole star in the night before it goes under!

5 The warm wind is still trying to connect things, the Catholic.

6 I am very much an isolated case. I have no patience. Our poor brother Godrewardyou said of the world: it doesn't count.

7 We are travelling at high speed towards a star in the Milky Way. There is a great calm in the earth's face. My heart beats too fast. Otherwise all is well.

THE SECOND PSALM

1 Under a flesh-coloured sun that brightens the eastern sky four breaths after midnight, under a heap of wind that covers them in gusts as with shrouds, the meadows from Füssen to Passau spread their lust-for-life propaganda.

2 From time to time the trains full of milk and passengers cleave the wheatfield oceans; but around the thunderers the air stands still, the light between the great petrifacts, the noon over the motionless fields.

3 The figures in the fields, brown-chested monsters, wicked looking, work with slow movements for the pale-faces in the petrifacts, as laid down in the documents.

4 For God created the earth that it might bring bread, and

gave us those with brown chests that this might enter our stomachs, mixed with the milk from the cows which he created. But what is the wind for, glorious in the tree tops?

5 The wind makes the clouds, that there may be rain on the ploughland, that bread may come. Let us now make children out of our lusts, for the bread, that it may be devoured.

6 This is Summer. Scarlet winds excite the plains, the smells at the end of June grow boundless. Vast visions of teeth-gnashing naked men travel at great heights southward.

7 In the cottages the light of the nights is like salmon. The resurrection of the flesh is being celebrated.

THE THIRD PSALM

1 In July you fish my voice from the ponds. There is cognac in my veins. My hand is made of flesh.

2 The pond water tans my skin, I am hard as a hazel switch, I would be good for bed, ladies.

3 In the red sun on the stones I love the guitars; they are beasts' guts, the guitar sings like a beast, it munches little songs.

4 In July I have an affair with the sky, I call him Little Boy Blue, glorious, violet, he loves me. It's male love.

5 He goes pale when I torture my gut beast and imitate the red lechery of the fields as well as the sighing of cows when lovemaking.

11 The Later Devotions and the
First City Poems
1920–1925

TO MY MOTHER

And when she was finished they laid her in earth
Flowers growing, butterflies juggling over her . . .
She, so light, barely pressed the earth down
How much pain it took to make her as light as that!

MOUNTED ON THE FAIRGROUND'S MAGIC HORSES

Mounted on the fairground's magic horses
As among the children I pranced by –
Bucking hard, we raised our blissful faces
To the marvellous clear evening sky –
All the passers-by just stood there laughing
And I heard them say, exactly like my mother:
Oh, he's so different, he's so different
Oh, he's so very different from us.

Seated with the cream of our society
As I outline my unusual views
They keep staring, till I'm sweating slightly –
They don't sweat, it's one of their taboos –
And I see them sitting there and laughing
And I hear them say, exactly like my mother:
Oh, he's so different, he's so different
Oh, he's so very different from us.

Up to heaven as one day I'm flying
(And they'll let me in, you'll see they will)
I shall hear the blessed spirits crying:
He is here, our cup of bliss to fill!
Then they'll stare at me and burst out laughing
And I'll hear them say, exactly like my mother:
Oh, he's so different, he's so different
Oh, he's so very different from us.

BALLAD ON MANY SHIPS

1

Brown brackish water, where the derelict schooners
Lie around cankered and huddled all day.
With sails which, once white, are now dirty like shirt-tails
On worm-eaten masts that are bent with decay.
These ships have forgotten the art of sailing.
Dropsy now stirs their bloated insides.
In moonlight and wind, a latrine for the seagulls
Idly they rock on the salt-water tides.

2

How many left them? Unseemly to wonder
Anyway they've gone and their contracts run out
Yet it still occurs that someone arrives there
Who's prepared to sail on them without question or doubt.
He hasn't a cap, naked he swam there
He hasn't a face, he's thin as a rake.
Even this ship shudders at the way he is grinning
As he stands in the stern staring down into his wake.

3

For he did not come without company
Not out of the sky; there were sharks at his side.
By sharks he was all the way escorted
They will live with him wherever he may reside.
So he arrives, the last of the seducers
So they meet up in the full morning light
And from other ships one ship lurches away
Spewing salt from repentance, making water with fright.

4

He takes his last sail and cuts himself a jacket
He gets his midday fish out of the sea below
He lies in the sun; and then comes evening
In the bilge water he washes his big toe.

Now and again looking up at the milky heavens
Keeps track of the gulls he brings down with seaweed slings.
And these he feeds every day to the sharks
Thus appeasing them mornings and evenings.

5

Oh, as he cruises with the trade winds behind him!
He lies in the halyards: decaying, an eel
And the sharks often listen to the song he's singing:
It's a song at the stake he is singing, they feel.
But on an evening in the month of October
After they had heard no song that day
He appeared in the stern, and they heard him saying:
What? 'Tomorrow we go down', they heard him say.

6

And the following night he lies in the halyards
Sleeps in the ropes, always his custom at night
When he suddenly senses a new ship is coming
And he looks down and sees her, clear in the moonlight.
And he takes courage, grins and climbs aboard her
He doesn't look round, but he combs his hair
To seem handsome. Suppose the new mistress
Is worse than this mistress, what will he care?

7

Not at all. He stands for a while at the taffrail
And he looks, and his lot it is to see
How the ship now sinks that was house and bed to him
And among the halyards the sharks swimming free . . .

8

And that's how he lives, the wind on his forehead
Always on ships worse than the last one has been
On so many ships, some half under water
And each month he changes his latrine.

Hatless and naked and with his own sharks too.
He knows his world. It is his home town.
He has a longing in him: for death by drowning
And he has a longing in him: not to go down.

BALLAD OF FRIENDSHIP

1

Like two pumpkins floating seaward
Decayed, but on a single stalk
In yellow rivers, they just drifted
And played at cards and played at talk
Shot at yellow moons and loved each other
Though their love was with averted eye:
  Remained as one many nights together
  And also: when the sun was high.

2

And when the sky, that beast, was clouded
Amid the hard green undergrowth
Like rancid dates they hung there dangling
Softly in each other's mouth.
And later, when their teeth were dropping
From their jaws, they avoided one another's eye:
  But remained as one many nights together
  And also: when the sun was high.

3

In the little shanty-like brothels
They satisfied their bodies' lust
Or in jungle glades behind the bushes
Shared the same girl when needs must.
But they washed their shirts in the morning
Arm in arm they walked and thigh to thigh:
  Joined as one many nights together
  And also: when the sun was high.

4

As on earth it grew colder
Roofless and bored they reclined
And among the other creepers they
Body to body lay entwined.
Talking together in the starlit evenings
Their words would sometimes pass each other by:
   Joined as one many nights together
   And also: when the sun was high.

5

But at last they came to an island
Where they both lived many a day
And when at last both wished to leave it
One there was could not get away.
And they watched the winds, the tides and the shipping
But each avoiding the other's eye:
   Joined as one many nights together
   And also: when the sun was high.

6

'Escape while you may, I am finished!
The salt tides eat into me so
Here I can still lie a little
For a week or two when you go.'
And a man lies ill by the water
Mutely he looks at a man nearby
   Who'd been with him many nights together
   And also: when the sun was high.

7

'I'm lying at my ease! O comrade, be off!'
'Let it be, comrade, there is no haste.'
'When the rains come, if you are not gone by then
We shall both of us rot and waste.'
So a shirt waves, and in salt wind stands a
Man watching the sea and the man nearby

Who'd been with him many nights together
    And also: when the sun was high.

8

And now came the day when they parted.
Spit out that date! It has withered away.
Nights it was winds they were watching
And one would be off the next day.
Still they walked together, shirts freshly washed
Arm in arm and smoking, thigh to thigh
    Joined as one many nights together
    And also: when the sun was high.

9

'O comrade, the wind fills the sails now!'
'The wind will blow till first light.'
'Comrade I beg you to tie me
To that tree there and bind my thighs tight.'
And the other man, smoking, then lashed him
Tight with cord to the tree nearby:
    Who'd been with him many nights together
    And also: when the sun was high.

10

'Comrade, the moon by clouds is covered!'
'The wind will disperse them and will wait for you.'
'Comrade, I'll watch as long as I can:
From this tree there's nothing to block the view.'
And days later, when the cord had been gnawed through
His eyes were still fixed on the sea moving by:
    During those last few nights he spent there
    And also: when the sun was high.

11

But the other, in weeks of sailing
On the sea, with women, in a glade:
While so many skies lost their colour
The man by the tree did not fade:

Their talks in the starlit nights together
Arm in arm and smoking, thigh to thigh
 Which still joined them, many nights together
 And also: when the sun was high.

BALLAD OF THE SECRETS OF ANY MAN AT ALL

1

You know what a man is. He's called by a name.
He walks in the street. He sits at the bar.
You can look at his face, you can listen to his voice.
A woman washed his shirt, a woman combs his hair.
 But strike him dead and it's no great loss
 If he never was more than the doer of his deed –
 Than the one who did what was bad to do
 And the one who did what was good.

2

And they know the skinless spot on his breast
And the bites on his neck they haven't forgot.
She knows, she bit him, she'll tell it to you
And the man with the skin: she has salt for the spot.
 But salt him down and it's no great loss
 If he weeps, throw him out on the garbage dump
 Before he has time to tell you who he is.
 If he asks for silence, stop his tongue!

3

And yet he has something at the bottom of his heart
That his friend does not know and his foe does not
And his angel not, nor does he himself:
If you cry when he dies, you're not mourning for that.
 And forget all about him and it's no great loss
 Because you are wrong, you've been fooled indeed.
 For he was never the man you knew
 And he was the doer of more than his deed.

4

Oh who childishly crams his bread in his mouth
With his earth-covered hands and laughs with each bite:
That shark-look from those strange-skinned eyes
Made the animals go pale with fright.
  But laugh with him! And wish him luck!
  And let him live! Even help him, too!
  Oh, he isn't good – you can count on that –
  But you don't know yet what will be done to you.

5

You who throw him into dirty-yellow seas
Or into the black earth dig him down
More than you knew will swim towards the fishes
And more than you buried will rot in the ground.
  But go ahead, bury him, it's no great loss
  For the grass that he walked on, and paid no heed
  When he trampled it down, wasn't there for the bull.
  And the doer doesn't live for the deed.

THOSE LOST SIGHT OF THEMSELVES

1

Those lost sight of themselves.
Each forgot who he was. The sea washed up
His corpse on some reef or other, pleasing the birds there
That could live on it for a few more weeks.
Many helplessly hid in night, believing they were
Invisible if they saw nothing. The night
Gave them cover and nonchalantly
Maternally stroking their faces took
Their vision away in silence. Amid wind and water sounds
They became lamenting voices, scarecrows to birds
And spooks to children, billowing shirts in the passage
Trembling for fear of laughter . . .

2
And already there rises
Laughing in the wind, another race:
Sleepers in the dark, eaters of birds
At one with their bodies
And lords of ineffable pleasure.

3
And on the sighs of those
On laughter and downfall
The sun feeds, the night drinks her fill.
So hourly death and devouring renew
That endless sensation
Ordained for the meek and those that are pure in heart:
To be young with exuberance and to age with relish.

GERMANY, YOU BLOND PALE CREATURE

Germany, you blond pale creature
With wild clouds and a gentle brow
What happened in your silent skies?
You have become the carrion pit of Europe.

Vultures over you!
Beasts tear your good body
The dying smear you with their filth
And their water
Wets your fields. Fields!

How gentle your rivers once
Now poisoned by purple anilin.
With their bare teeth children root
Your cereals up, they're
Hungry.

But the harvest floats into the
Stinking water.

Germany, you blond pale creature
Neverneverland. Full of
Departed souls. Full of dead people.
Nevermore nevermore will it beat –
Your heart, which has gone
Mouldy, which you have sold
Pickled in chili saltpetre
In exchange
For flags.

Oh carrion land, misery hole!
Shame strangles the remembrance of you
And in the young men whom
You have not ruined
America awakens.

THREE FRAGMENTS

2

When I saw the world had died away/ the plants, the human
race and all other surviving creatures of the surface of the
earth and the deep sea-floor/ a mountain grew/ bigger than
the other mountains and high Himalaya/ and it used up the
whole world as it grew/ and wisdom gave it a great hump
and a greater was made by stupidity/ light strengthened it but
darkness made it still greater/ thus the world transformed
itself into one single mountain so that it could be said this is
the greatest/

4

The seventh night I observed a man squatting on a stone
latrine/ in his hands he held two goblets and mixed a drink
and the drink was very fierce/ and he poured the contents of
the goblets incessantly from one to the other/ yet without
losing a drop as he did so/ and all living things fled from him
on account of the stink which was very strong/ only a lioness

stood uninterruptedly by his knee/ however he did not look
at her being entirely occupied with his drink which did not
diminish/ I am writing this down because I like precision/

7

A boy too ran beside me and I didn't chase him away/ on the
contrary he kept coming back like a fly and sang as he fled
before me/ but his voice was very loud/ and he observed me
incessantly even when I ate and as he observed me he grew
fat yet did not eat and I grew thin/ often however I reckoned
by the stones how long I could stand having that boy observe
me while we crossed the desert and I chased him away/ but
one day on the plain beneath our feet a strong light appeared
whose source was unknown and the boy shouted after me as
if he could not see me went two paces and disappeared/

BORN LATER

I admit it: I
Have no hope.
The blind talk of a way out. I
See.

When the errors have been used up
As our last companion, facing us
Sits nothingness

AS I WELL KNOW

As I well know
The impure journey hellwards
Across the whole of Heaven.
They are driven in carriages, transparent:
This, they are told, beneath you
Is Heaven.

I do know they are told this
For I imagine
Precisely they include
Many who would not be able to recognise it, for precisely they
Thought it would be more radiant.

THE BREAD AND THE CHILDREN

1
They did not eat the bread
Kept in the wooden box
But shouted that instead
They wanted to eat rocks.

2
The bread therefore went mouldy.
Uneaten there it lay
And looking skywards mildly
It heard the larder say:

3
'One day will come a crisis
When for a crust they'll fight
Heightened with just some spices
To still their appetite.'

4
The children had departed
On distant roads to roam
Leading to lands uncharted
And outside Christendom.

5
The heathen saw children starving
Their faces shrivelled and wan.
The heathen gave them nothing
But let them hunger on.

6

Now there has come a crisis
And for a crust they'll fight
Heightened with just some spices
To still their appetite.

7

But the bread's been fed to the cattle
It mouldered and went dry.
So pray God, keep a little
Spice for them in the sky.

OBSERVATION BEFORE THE PHOTOGRAPH OF
THERESE MEIER

Back home, at my place, on the flea-yellowish wallpaper
Under the haunt of visiting moths, the stuffed vulture:
Forgotten by the last tenant or perhaps turned over
To me, the picture of the departed spinster Therese Meier.

It is really only a photograph and badly faded
And I don't know: is it a good likeness of her?
I honour it out of piety and because we are somehow suited.
Sticky with sweat as I am, drunk on the black leather sofa.

It is black lacquered, glass-fronted, a plastic frame
Rather old, virgin Meier, compared to the wallpaper
Not quite so pretty, but the black thing is a prop to me just
        the same
I would feel contempt for myself if I should ever . . .

And even so it is only a question of how long:
The glass anyway would bring in a few pfennigs for kirsch
And the photo looks as if its liver had sort of gone wrong
And every evening its paper has a paler smirch.

Perhaps some day that white paper will be the one thing
        grinning there
And I will have to say to myself: once more you're too late,
        chum.
Kirsch is an ally against contempt. But I don't really care
To do it. Matter with me of so much gone over the dam.

SENTIMENTAL SONG NO. 78

Oh it was a night of loving
And I slept exhaustedly:
And I saw the greenness budding
In the sunshine on a tree.

And I thought, as I lay dreaming
Of the sunshine on that tree:
Underneath its branches greening
Let them one day bury me.

Waking then in spotless linen
With you lying next to me
I thought: here's the shroud so clean in
Which I'll have them bury me.

And the moon came softly streaming
Through the curtains on to me
And I lay quite silent, dreaming
When my burial would be.

Feeling then your warmth beside me
Little body, thigh and knee
In these arms, I thought, I'll hide me
Here's where they can bury me.

Like expectant heirs I saw you
Round my bed weep many a tear.

If, I thought, I die tomorrow
They must let me disappear.

You gave much: I'll make you sorry
That you didn't give the lot:
And the malice you folk bore me –
Will be something you'll regret.

ON THE PLEASURES OF DRINK

1
In the greenish hugger-mugger
With his bottle sits a bugger
Swigging schnapps. (Swigging schnapps.)
With his bottle sits a bugger near collapse.
(Near collapse.)

2
Look, chaste Josef though dumbfounded
By great mounds of flesh surrounded
Sits content. (Sits content.)
Sucks his fingers which are chaste and innocent.
(Innocent.)

3
Seven stars can taste too bitter.
Gentle plucking on the zither
Puts that right. (Puts that right.)
Seven songs and seven litres, you show fight.
(You show fight.)

4
Linsel Klopps walked straight and steady
Now feels freer as instead he
Walks askew. (Walks askew.)
And, oh swan, to you already thanks are due.
(Thanks are due.)

EXEMPLARY CONVERSION OF A GROG-SELLER

1

Bottles, glasses, on the bar behind him
Heavy-lidded, lips of violet
Dreary eyes in his perspiring features
Sits a grog-seller pallid and fat.
His greasy fingers count the money
Pushing coins into a heap:
Then in an oily pool of gin he
Drops his head and falls asleep.

2

And his body heaves, he writhes there groaning
Cold sweat smears his forehead like slime
While in his spongelike brain there enter
Nightmare figures as in pantomime.
And he dreams: he is in heaven
And must go where God's enthroned
He because the thought unmans him
Drinks till he's completely stoned.

3

Seven angels form a ring around him
And he starts to stagger on his feet
But the publican is led reluctant
Speechless to God's judgement seat.
He can't raise his heavy eyelids
Of God's white light he stands in dread
Feels his tongue is blue and stuck there
Weighing in his mouth like lead.

4

And he looks round in search of rescue
And he sees in green and seaweed light:
Fourteen orphan children floating slowly
Downstream, faces fading ashen white.

And he says: it's only seven.
Being drunk I see them twice.
Cannot say it, since his tongue is
Firmly held as in a vice.

5
And he looks round in search of rescue
Sees men who play poker all day long
And he bawls: I am your friend the grog-seller!
They go on bawling their drunken song.
And they bawl that their salvation
Lies in whisky or in gin.
And he sees their pale green blotches:
Putrefaction has set in.

6
And he looks round in search of rescue
And he finds: I'm not wearing what I think.
I'm in underpants in heaven! Hears their question:
Did you sell off all your clothes for drink?
And he says: I did have clothes once.
And they say: Don't you feel shame?
And he knows: Many have stood here
Whom I have stripped of all but name.

7
And he no longer looks for rescue
And he kneels so quickly his knees crack
And he feels the sword where neck meets body
And the shirt sweat-damp against his back:
And he feels the scorn in heaven
And deep within he is aware:
Because I am a grog-seller
God has banished me from there.

8
Then he wakes: though with eyes still bleary
Heavy-lidded, lips of violet.

But he tells himself: No longer will I
Be a grog-seller pallid and fat.
Rather will I seek out orphan children
Drunks, the old, the chronic ill
They alone shall henceforth get this
Filthy lucre from the till.

OF THE SEDUCED GIRLS

1
Down to the shallow ponds, gone brown and muddy
The devil will take me in my declining days
To show me the remains of many a waterlogged body
That upon my guilty conscience weighs.

2
Under sad dull skies they all proceeded
Loose and lethargic floating down to hell
Massed together like entangled seaweed
Hoping to put their stay there on my bill.

3
Earlier, their slack infected bodies had provided
Fuel for a blaze I myself fanned alight
But those who savoured the orange day beside me
Cut themselves off from the murky night.

4
Superbly fed, at ease and that much fuller
They idly left me for the flames of guilt to scorch
Messed up the earth for me, made the sky yet duller
Leaving me an infected body and no debauch.

THE SHIPWRECKED MAN'S REPORT

When the ship was wrecked
I went into the waters. The water's force
Flung me up on a bare and narrow rock.
I lost consciousness at once.
Meanwhile my world went down. However
My hair had already dried
When I awoke.

I ate something out of shells
And slept in a tree
(My best time) for three days
And I *went* far
As I had nothing but space.

I touched nothing with my hand.
I had not seen the view before.
After three nights I recognised
The moon once more.

I hung a rag in a tree
And stood by it all day
Till the next day broke.
The water was calm.
In my rag no breath stirred
No ship came
No birds appeared.

Later I did see ships
Five times I saw sails
Three times smoke.

EVERY YEAR

1
Now, in this night in which I love you
White clouds skim across the heavens without a sound
And the waters snarl over the pebbles
And the wind shudders along the barren ground.

2
White waters go trickling
Downhill every year.
Up in the heavens
The clouds are always there.

3
Later, when the years grow lonely
Clouds, white clouds, will still be found.
And the waters will snarl over the pebbles
And the wind shudder along the barren ground.

I HAD NEVER LOVED YOU SO MUCH

I had never loved you so much, ma soeur
As I did leaving you in that sunset.
The wood, the blue wood swallowed me, ma soeur
And over it pale stars already hung in the West.

I can tell you I laughed a lot, ma soeur
As I played a game against darkening fate –
Meanwhile the faces were fading behind me
Slowly in the blue wood, its twilight.
Everything was beautiful, ma soeur, for one sunset
As it had never been, never again would be –
Though all that I have left of it is the great
Evening birds hungering in the dark sky.

BALLAD OF HANNAH CASH

1

With her thin cotton skirt and her yellow shawl
And her eyes twin pools of jet
And no talent or money, she still had it all
From her hair like a clear black waterfall
To her toes that were blacker yet:
  Yes, that was Hannah Cash, my friend
  Who made the toffs pay through the nose.
  With the wind she came and with the wind she went
  As across the savannahs it blows.

2

She hadn't a blouse and she hadn't a hat
As for hymns to sing, she had still fewer.
She washed into the city like a half-drowned cat
A little grey creature that clawed and spat
Thrust with corpses in a black sewer.
  She washed the glasses clean of absinthe
  Herself she never got clean
  You ask, was Hannah Cash pure, my friend?
  I'd say she must have been.

3

One night she went to the Sailors' Bar
With her eyes twin pools of jet
And found J. Kent of the moleskin hair –
Yes, Slasher Jack from the Sailors' Bar
Who took what he could get.
  Straightway Kent's eyes began to flash
  As he picked his scabby nose:
  Those eyes, my friend, shook Hannah Cash
  Right down to the tip of her toes.

4

They 'found common ground' between fish and game
And it made them 'companions for life'.

They themselves had no table, no fish or game
They hadn't a bed, nor had they a name
For any children who might arrive.
   The blizzards can howl, it can rain without end
   The savannah can flood far and wide
   But Hannah Cash's place, my friend
   Is by her husband's side.

5

The milk woman says he can't walk erect
The sheriff calls him a rat.
But Hannah says: you are correct
He is my man. If you don't object
I'll stick by him. Because of that.
   He may be lame, he may be mad
   He may beat her as he will:
   All that worries Hannah Cash, my lad
   Is – does she love him still?

6

No roof above the cot was there
Nothing mild in the parents' manners.
Never apart, year after year
From the city to the forests went that pair
From the forests to the savannahs.
   When winds are cold and blizzards wild
   You keep moving as long as you can.
   So long did Hannah Cash, my child
   Move onwards with her man.

7

No one so poorly dressed as she
She never had a Sunday fling
No trips to pastrycooks for tea
No wheaten cakes in Lent for three
No choir in which to sing.

And every day might be as sad
As every other one:
On the darkest days Hannah Cash, my lad
Was always bathed in sun.

8
She stole the salt, the fishes he.
That's all. Such heroism.
And as she cooks those fishes, see
The children sitting on his knee
Learning their catechism.
　　Through fifty years of night and wind
　　They shared each other's bed.
　　Yes, that was Hannah Cash, my friend
　　God rest her weary head.

BALLAD OF THE LOVE-DEATH

1
Eaten away by black rain seven times over
A sordid mouth which gollops down their love
With muslin curtains damp as shrouds for cover:
Such is the attic which they'll never leave.

2
Leprous the wallpaper, mildewed and crumbling!
Shut in by wooden boards they're welded, tight:
To this white couple in its heavenly coupling
The threadbare heaven seems a sheer delight.

3
To start with he'll sit there in damp towels, chewing
The black cheroots she gives him. Mouth askew
He'll kill the time nodding his head, and cooing
With drooping eyelid that he loves her true.

4

Such hairiness, she feels, and oh, such wisdom!
He sees the day dissolve, his eyes a slot
While, green as soap, the clouds shut off the sky's dome
And all he thinks is: how my shirt will rot.

5

They're pouring brandy down their dried-up bodies
He's feeding her on evening's pale green light
And now her thighs are covered with red blotches
And now her face is slowly going white.

6

She's like some waterlogged field by the river
(They're deaf, they're orphaned, all their flesh is drained!)
He wants his sleep, but will she let him leave her?
Green sky above, that recently has rained!

7

The second day they used the sweat-stained curtains
As stiffened sheets to wrap their corpses in
And packed their thighs with greasy strips of shirting
Because they've learned that's where the chills begin.

8

And, oh, love stabbed them through and through, so neatly
As when God's hailstones through the water hiss.
And deep within them, gutting them completely
And thick as yeast, welled up green bitterness.

9

Their hair filled with the smells of sweat and urine
They'll never see again the break of day.
Yet, years from now, the day will come and pour in
To that wallpaper vault, bestial and grey.

10

Oh, her young pearly body, soft as butter!
Beaten so raw by wood and love right through
Dissolves like wood in some old battered cutter
Beneath a storm. Like grass soggy with dew.

11

Oh, but the hand that holds her breast is grassy!
And black the stench of plague in every limb!
Mild air rinsed down the window, hard and glassy
While still the rotten cupboard sheltered them.

12

Like dishwater the evening rinsed the skylight
Its curtains mangy with tobacco smoke.
Across green seas two lovers in the twilight
Drift, soaked in love, like some rain-sodden hulk

13

Which, breaking up deep in the tropic oceans
Hangs there between seaweed and the pallid fish
And, far below, starts gentle rocking motions
Caught from the surface where the salt winds swish.

14

On the fourth morning neighbours got up, fetched their
Thundering sledgehammers and smashed down the door
They heard the silence, saw the corpses stretched there
(And murmured saying what a greenish glare

15

Can come from faces); what is more, the bed kept
Its smell of love, the window burst with frost:
A corpse is such a cold thing! And a thread crept
Thin, cold and black, towards them from its breast.

GREAT HYMN OF THANKSGIVING

1

Worship the night and the darkness by which you're
surrounded!
Come with a shove
Look to the heaven above:
Day is already confounded.

2

Worship the grass and the beasts that have life and must
perish!
Lo! Grass and beasts
Like you partake of life's feasts
Like you they also must perish.

3

Worship the tree that from carrion soars up towards heaven!
Worship the rot
Worship the tree it begot
But furthermore worship heaven.

4

Worship with fulness of heart the weak memory of heaven!
It cannot trace
Either your name or your face
Nobody knows you're still living.

5

Worship the cold and the dark and calamity dire!
Scan the whole earth:
You're a thing of no worth
And you may calmly expire.

OF BAD TEETH

1

Toothless from much blackberry-gobbling
Fang-snarling and empty squabbling
A child in innocence, chaste as a sage
Here's how I spend my middle age.

2

I can crush stones with my jaw, it's true
But the flesh of my gums is slatey blue.
Is that why I chew on them, then, each day
And put my stomach on public display?

3

I was poor, yet the women were round me like flies
But since I've had these rotting cavities
In my mouth, they don't think I'm a chap
Who can rip his meat up with a savage snap.

4

For years I had plenty of teeth in my jaw
Which not one of those bitches was grateful for.
Now their picture of me is blurred I see
My teeth did everything for me.

5

Despised and nasty, I grew colder each year
And restricted myself to the metaphysical sphere.
Shunned by myself, I've seen me fall
An utter victim to alcohol.

THOSE DAYS OF MY YOUTH

Those days of my youth! Let me remember
(Only note how fast the memory goes).

Flimsy shadows. Walls with white distemper.
Nickelodeon *couleur de rose.*

Apple-clear the ponds where we went carping
Sinuous waters, buoyant greedy guts
Then at night the bowler-hatted larking
All of us in raspberry-coloured shirts.

Oh the harsh snarl of guitar strings roaring!
Heavenly distensions of our throats!
Trousers stiff with dirt and love! Such whoring!
Long green slimy nights: we were like stoats.

Lounging sleepily beneath the willows
Oh tobacco, apple-green sky above!
Flying like pigeons drunk on kirsch, poor fellows –
Ending limper than a worn-out glove.

Tender joint of lamb in fresh starched linen
Watch out, the good shepherd's on his way!
You may safely graze, and fill the skin in
Which your red heart sits, soon to decay.

PSALM

1 We didn't bat an eyelid when the white waters rose to our
necks;

2 We smoked cigars as the dark brown evenings gnawed at
us;

3 We didn't say no when we drowned in the sky.

4 The waters didn't tell anyone that they were up to our
necks;

5 There was nothing in the newspapers about our not saying anything;

6 The sky doesn't hear the cries of people who are drowning.

7 So we sat on the big stones like lucky people;

8 So we killed the greenfinches which talked about our silent faces.

9 Who talks about the stones?

10 And who wants to know what waters, evenings, and sky mean to us?

THE FOURTH PSALM

1 What do people still expect of me?
I have played all the patiences, spat out all the kirsch
Stuffed all the books into the stove
Loved all the women till they stank like Leviathan.
Truly I am a great saint, my ear is so rotten it will soon drop off.
So why is there no peace? Why do the people stand in the yard like rubbish bins – waiting for something to be put into them?
I have made it plain it is no use any more to expect the Song of Songs from me.
I have set the police on the buyers.
Whoever it is you are looking for, it is not me.

2 I am the most practical of all my brothers –
And it all starts in *my* head!
My brothers were cruel, I am the cruellest
And it is *I* who weep at night!

3 When the tables of the law broke, so did all vices.
Even sleeping with one's sister is no fun any more.
Murder is too much trouble for many
Writing poems is too common
Since everything is too uncertain
Many prefer to tell the truth
Being ignorant of the danger.
The courtesans pickle meat for the winter
And the devil no longer carries away his best people.

Five Epistles

FIRST LETTER TO THE HALFBREEDS, AFTER AN
EMBITTERED COMPLAINT AGAINST INCLEMENCY

I am quite convinced that it will be a fine day tomorrow
That sunshine follows rain
That my neighbour loves his daughter
And my enemy is a bad man.
Also that I am better off than almost anyone else
I do not doubt.
Also I have never been heard to say
Things used to be better, or
The human race is degenerating
Or there are no women one man can satisfy.
In all this
I am broader-minded, more trusting and politer than the
      discontented
For all this
Seems to me to prove very little.

TO THE MAN-EATERS. LETTERS
TO THE MUSCOVITES – I

One shouldn't be too critical
Between yes and no
There's not such a great difference.
Writing on white paper
Is a good thing, so are
Sleeping and having one's evening meal.
Water fresh on the skin, the wind
Pleasant clothes
The ABC
Opening the bowels.

In the house of the hanged man it is not
Proper to talk about the noose.
And in the muck
To find a sharp distinction between
Clay and marl
Is not appropriate.
Ah
Anyone who can conceive
Of a starry heaven
Really should keep his mouth shut.

SECOND LETTER TO THE MUSCOVITES,
A FURTHER ADMONITION

Someone may turn up from Tiflis and kill me off.
Then a day goes pale in the air
The trembling of a few blades of grass, which I noticed long
        ago
Comes finally to an end.
A dead man whose friend I was
Has nobody left who knows what he looked like.
My tobacco smoke
Which meanwhile has been climbing through a myriad
        heavens
Loses its faith in God
And
Climbs on.

EPISTLE TO THE CHICAGOANS

The laughter on the slave markets of the continents
Formerly confined to yourselves
Must utterly have shaken you, the cold in the regions of the
        fourth depth
Will have soaked into your skin.

So you still love the horse thieves' blue eyes?
But when you are taken into the old people's home
I shall examine your backs to see
If the winters have marked you.
Your children
Will hear from me, on the evidence of your dead wrists
Whether you stood in the rivers
Between the ice floes and the black fishes
And learned something about this planet.
Oh, in reality there is nothing
But
Deceivers and deceived.
See?

EPISTLE ON SUICIDE

Killing oneself
Is a slight affair.
You can chat about it with your washerwoman.
Elucidate the pros and cons with a friend.
A certain sense of tragedy, however attractive
Is to be avoided.
Though there is no need to make a dogma of that.
But there is more to be said, I think
For the usual slight deception:
You're fed up with changing your linen or, better still
Your wife has been unfaithful
(This is a draw with people who get surprised by such things
And is not too high-flown.)
Anyway
It should not seem
As if one had put
Too high a value on oneself.

ONCE I THOUGHT

Once I thought I'd like to die between sheets of my own
Now
I no longer straighten the pictures on the wall
I let the shutters rot, open my bedroom to the rain
Wipe my mouth on another man's napkin.
I had a room for four months without ever knowing
That its window had a view to the back of the house (though
        that's something I love)
Because I so favour the provisional and don't altogether
        believe in myself.
Therefore I take any lodging, and if I shiver I say:
I'm still shivering.
And so engrained is this attitude
That it allows me none the less to change my linen
Out of courtesy to the ladies and because
One surely won't
Need linen for ever.

REPORT ELSEWHITHER

When I entered the new-built
Cities many came with me, but
When I left the new-built cities not one
Left with me.
On the day appointed for
The fight, I went out to fight
And stood from morning till evening
And saw no one stand by me
But many watched, smiling
Or weeping, from the walls.

I thought, they've forgotten
The day they appointed
Or they've chosen some other day

And forgotten to tell me.
But at evening I looked up and saw them
Sitting on the wall eating
And
What they were eating was stones
And I saw they had cleverly
Learned to eat a new kind of food
Just in time.

And I saw in their eyes
That the enemy was not fighting me, but that shots
Hailed down on the spot where
I stood. So I smiled and went away
From that spot.

Off we went then, friend and foe
To drink wine together and smoke
And they kept telling me
Throughout that fine night
That they had nothing against me
No word of mine had
Hurt them, as I'd supposed
For they'd not understood one of them
Only they'd got the impression
That I wanted something which they
Had – something appointed
And forever sacred
But I smiled and assured them
I wanted nothing of the kind.

SONG OF THE RUINED
INNOCENT FOLDING LINEN

1
What my mother told me
Cannot be true, I'm sure.

She said: when once you're sullied
You'll never again be pure.
  That doesn't apply to linen
  And it doesn't apply to me.
  Just dip it in the river
  And it's clean instantly.

2

At eleven I was sinful
As any army bride.
In fact at only fourteen
My flesh I mortified.
  The linen was greying already
  I dipped it in the stream.
  In the basket it lies chastely
  Just like a maiden's dream.

3

Before my first man knew me
I had already fallen.
I stank to heaven, truly
A scarlet Babylon.
  Swirled in a gentle curve
  The linen in the river
  Feels at the touch of the wave:
  I'm growing slowly whiter.

4

For when my first man embraced me
And I embraced him
I felt the wicked urges fly
From my breast and from my womb.
  That's how it is with linen
  And it's how it was with me.
  The waters rush past swiftly
  And all the dirt cries: see!

5

But when the others came
That was a dismal spring.
They called me wicked names
And I became a wicked thing.
   No woman can restore herself
   By storing herself away.
   If linen lies long on the shelf
   On the shelf it will go grey.

6

Once more there came another
As another year began.
When everything was other, I saw
I was another woman.
   Dip it in the river and shake it!
   There's sun and bleach and air!
   Use it and let them take it:
   It will be fresh as before!

7

I know: much more can happen
Till there's nothing to come at the last.
It's only when it's never been used
That linen has gone to waste.
   And once it is brittle
   No river can wash it pure.
   It will be rinsed away in tatters.
   That day will come for sure.

AN INSCRIPTION TOUCHES OFF
SENTIMENTAL MEMORIES

1

Among those yellowed sheets that mattered once to me
(You drink, then read; it's better when you're pissed)

A photograph. Inscribed on which I see
The words PURE, LUCID, EVIL, through a mist.

2
She always used to wash with almond soap
The small rough towel was hers as well
And the Tokay recipe and the Javanese pipe
To cover up love's smell.

3
She took it seriously. She didn't float. She was thoughtful.
Art, in her view, demanded sacrifice.
She loved love, not her lover; no one could pull
The wool over her eyes.

4
She laughed, passiveness put up her back
As for her head, that was screwed on all right
She had a cold shoulder, and the knack:
Thinking of it I start to sweat with fright.

5
That was her. My God, I wish I had
An inscription like that on my tombstone: Here lies B.B.
PURE, LUCID, EVIL.
I'd sleep all right with that on top of me.

NOT THAT I DIDN'T ALWAYS

Not that I didn't always have the very best of intentions
An undue fondness for tobacco is perhaps the one fault I could
        mention
Or that I didn't perhaps get upset when it was much too late
        to be
And Müllereisert always said: come on, stop all that sipping
        of thin tea.

But my principle was: anyone can run into luck, you just
        mustn't run away
And suddenly it turned out that I'd written a real play.

I'd hardly noticed a thing, it had just sort of slid out
Matters of principle have always given me a lot to worry about
For me everything started with principles, I'd say
Tobacco, for instance, as well as my taste for liquor
I really did want to keep quiet at first, but I gave myself away
And Orge said: well, it's not going to get better any quicker
Best thing would be to finish yourself off now with a bullet
Rather than suffer at length, or however the consolatory
        phrases put it.

And now almost every week I write one
It tastes like soft-boiled eggs in a glass
I know that one is more than none
But I think it's all tied up with my aquiline nose, you know
And you just can't do anything about it – that was proved
        long ago
And I too was born to rise to the highest positions.
Orge once inadvertently let drop the view:
You used to have the makings of a tiger in you
But you had better say goodbye to such ambitions.

ON HIS MORTALITY

1

Smoke your cigars: that was my doctor's comforting answer!
With or without them one day we'll end up with the under-
        taker.
In the membrane of my eye for example there are signs of
        cancer
From which I shall die sooner or later.

2

Naturally one need not be discouraged for that reason
For years such a man may carry on.
He can stuff his body with chicken and blackberry in season
Though naturally one day he'll be gone.

3

Against this there's nothing one can contrive either with
        schnapps or sharp practice
Such a cancer grows subtly; one feels nothing inside.
And perhaps you are written off when the fact is
You are just standing at the altar with your bride.

4

My uncle for example wore trousers with knife-edge creases
Though long selected to go elsewhere.
His cheeks were still ruddy but they were churchyard roses
And on him was not one healthy hair.

5

There are families in which it is hereditary
But they never admit it nor condemn.
They can distinguish pineapple from rosemary
But their cancer may be a hernia to them.

6

My grandfather, though, knew what lay ahead and made no
        query
And was prudent, punctiliously doing what the doctor said.
And he even attained the age of fifty before becoming weary.
One day of such a life is more than a dog would have led.

7

Our sort know: no point being envious.
Each man has his cross to bear, I fear.
Kidney trouble is my particular curse
I've not had a drink in more than a year.

SONG OF THE ROSES ON THE SHIPKA PASS

One Sunday comes back to me from my childhood
With Father singing in his mellow bass
Across the glasses and the empty bottles
His song 'The Roses on the Shipka Pass'.

Sunday came round again, and once more Father
Was singing to us in his mellow bass
He didn't sing of lilies or of lilac
He sang of roses on the Shipka Pass.

And often thus, tears trickling down his whiskers
Father sang to us in his mellow bass
Singing not of the roses at Mycenae
But of the roses on the Shipka Pass.

Full often sleep lay heavy on our eyelids
While Father's still were dewy as the grass
From his last rendering, as once more he gave us
His song 'The Roses on the Shipka Pass'.

His grave was being dug for him already
But still he sang, on, sinking though he was
That while for his part he might be forgotten
There'd still be roses on the Shipka Pass.

ON THE INFANTICIDE MARIE FARRAR

1
Marie Farrar: month of birth, April
An orphaned minor; rickets; birthmarks, none; previously
Of good character, admits that she did kill
Her child as follows here in summary.
She visited a woman in a basement
During her second month, so she reported

And there was given two injections
Which, though they hurt, did not abort it.
　　But you I beg, make not your anger manifest
　　For all that lives needs help from all the rest.

2

But nonetheless, she says, she paid the bill
As was arranged, then bought herself a corset
And drank neat spirit, peppered it as well
But that just made her vomit and disgorge it.
Her belly now was noticeably swollen
And ached when she washed up the plates.
She says that she had not finished growing.
She prayed to Mary, and her hopes were great.
　　You too I beg, make not your anger manifest
　　For all that lives needs help from all the rest.

3

Her prayers, however, seemed to be no good.
She'd asked too much. Her belly swelled. At Mass
She started to feel dizzy and she would
Kneel in a cold sweat before the Cross.
Still she contrived to keep her true state hidden
Until the hour of birth itself was on her
Being so plain that no one could imagine
That any man would ever want to tempt her.
　　But you I beg, make not your anger manifest
　　For all that lives needs help from all the rest.

4

She says that on the morning of that day
While she was scrubbing stairs, something came clawing
Into her guts. It shook her once and went away.
She managed to conceal her pain and keep from crying.
As she, throughout the day, hung up the washing
She racked her brain, then realised in fright

She was going to give birth. At once a crushing
Weight grabbed at her heart. She didn't go upstairs till night.
  And yet I beg, make not your anger manifest
  For all that lives needs help from all the rest.

5
But just as she lay down they fetched her back again:
Fresh snow had fallen, and it must be swept.
That was a long day. She worked till after ten.
She could not give birth in peace till the household slept.
And then she bore, so she reports, a son.
The son was like the son of any mother.
But she was not like other mothers are – but then
There are no valid grounds why I should mock her.
  You too I beg, make not your anger manifest
  For all that lives needs help from all the rest.

6
So let her finish now and end her tale
About what happened to the son she bore
(She says there's nothing she will not reveal)
So men may see what I am and you are.
She'd just climbed into bed, she says, when nausea
Seized her. Never knowing what should happen till
It did, she struggled with herself to hush her
Cries, and forced them down. The room was still.
  And you I beg, make not your anger manifest
  For all that lives needs help from all the rest.

7
The bedroom was ice cold, so she called on
Her last remaining strength and dragged her-
Self out to the privy and there, near dawn
Unceremoniously, she was delivered
(Exactly when, she doesn't know). Then she
Now totally confused, she says, half froze

And found that she could scarcely hold the child
For the servants' privy lets in the heavy snows.
  And you I beg, make not your anger manifest
  For all that lives needs help from all the rest.

8

Between the servants' privy and her bed (she says
That nothing happened until then), the child
Began to cry, which vexed her so, she says
She beat it with her fists, hammering blind and wild
Without a pause until the child was quiet, she says.
She took the baby's body into bed
And held it for the rest of the night, she says
Then in the morning hid it in the laundry shed.
  But you I beg, make not your anger manifest
  For all that lives needs help from all the rest.

9

Marie Farrar: month of birth, April
Died in the Meissen penitentiary
An unwed mother, judged by the law, she will
Show you how all that lives, lives frailly.
You who bear your sons in laundered linen sheets
And call your pregnancies a 'blessed' state
Should never damn the outcast and the weak:
Her sin was heavy, but her suffering great.
  Therefore, I beg, make not your anger manifest
  For all that lives needs help from all the rest.

BALLAD OF THE OLD WOMAN

Last Monday she got up about eleven
They never thought she'd make it on her own
She took her fever as a sign from heaven
For months she'd been no more than skin and bone.

For two whole days she'd vomited saliva
And looked as white as snow when she got up
Weeks back the priest had called to anoint and shrive her
Coffee, it seemed, was all she cared to sup.

Once more, though, she'd evaded death's caresses
The final rites had been mistimed a bit
She loved the walnut chest that held her dresses
And could not bring herself to part from it.

Old furniture is often worm-infested
But still it's part of you. And so to speak
She would have missed it. Well, may God protect it.
She made twelve pots of blackberry jam last week.

What's more, she's now made sure her teeth are working.
You eat much better if your teeth are right
You wear them in the morning when out walking
And keep them in old coffee cups at night.

Her children have remembered her existence
She's heard from them, and God will guard them. Yes
She'll last the winter out with God's assistance
Nor is there much wrong with her old black dress.

MORNING ADDRESS TO A TREE NAMED GREEN

1
Green, I owe you an apology.
I couldn't sleep last night because of the noise of the storm.
When I looked out I noticed you swaying
Like a drunken ape. I remarked on it.

2
Today the yellow sun is shining in your bare branches.
You are shaking off a few tears still, Green.

But now you know your own worth.
You have fought the bitterest fight of your life.
Vultures were taking an interest in you.
And now I know: it's only by your inexorable
Flexibility that you are still upright this morning.

3

In view of your success it's my opinion today:
It was no mean feat to grow up so tall
In between the tenements, so tall, Green, that
The storm can get at you as it did last night.

THE LORD OF THE FISH

1

Ah, he did not come like the moon
At fixed times, yet like her he departed.
Preparing his simple meal for him
Was not hard.

2

When he was there, for one evening
There was one amongst them
Expecting little, greatly giving
Unknown to all and close to everyone.

3

They were accustomed to his going
His coming astonished them
And yet he always comes back, resembling
The moon, in a good mood – again.

4

Sits and talks like them: of their affairs
The women's doings, how the fish will sell
When to go to sea, the cost of nets
And how to save taxes most of all.

5

And though he never contrived
To remember their names
Where their work was concerned
He knew all sorts of things.

6

When he spoke so of their affairs
They in their turn would ask: what of your own?
And he would look round smiling on all sides
And hesitantly say: got none.

7

And so with talking back and forth
He kept company with them.
He did not eat more than his worth
Although he always came unbidden.

8

Sooner or later someone will be asking:
Tell us, what brings you to us here?
He'll stand up hastily, surmising
A change of mood is in the air.

9

Politely, having nothing to offer them
A servant dismissed, he will go out.
No smallest shadow of him will remain
No hollow in the wicker seat.

10

But yet he will allow another man
To show himself the richer in his place
Indeed he will not hinder anyone
From speaking where he holds his peace.

ABOUT EXERTION

1

You smoke. You abuse yourself. You drink yourself senseless.
You sleep. You grin into a naked face.
Time's tooth, my dear fellow, is gnawing too slowly.
You smoke. You shit. You turn out some verse.

2

Unchastity and poverty are our professions
Unchastity sugared our innocent youth.
What a man has performed in God's good sunshine
Is what he atones for in God's good earth.

3

The mind made a whore of the body's delight
Since first unclenching hairy claws
The feel of the sun won't penetrate
That skin of parchment any more.

4

O you green islands in tropical seas
How do you look next morning without your make-up on?
The white hell of the visionaries
Is a wooden hut where the rain gets in.

5

How are we to knock our girls unconscious?
With sables' meats? No, gin would be better.
A lilac brew of potent punches
With drowned flies in to make it bitter.

6

You soak till you're taking perfume for liquor.
You hand round black coffee, the brandy also.
It's all of it useless, Maria; far quicker
To tan our exquisite skins with snow.

7

With the cynical charm of airy poems
Leaving an orange bitterness on the palate
Straight off the ice! Meanwhile with an eye on
Black Malayan hair! Oh tobacco opiate!

8

In wind-crazed hovels of Nanking paper
Oh you bitterness of the world's joys
When the moon, that mild white animal
Falls out of colder skies!

9

Oh heavenly fruit of the maculate conception!
When did anything perfect come your way, brother?
You take kirsch to wash down your own funeral procession
And little lanterns of airy paper.

10

Awake and hung over early next morning
A grin shows through teeth foul with nicotine stains.
And often we feel on the tongue as we're yawning
That bitter orange taste again.

SONG ON BLACK SATURDAY AT THE
ELEVENTH HOUR OF EASTER EVE

1

In spring between green skies and wild
Enamoured winds part animal already
I went down into the black cities
Papered inside with chilly words to say.

2

I filled myself with animals of asphalt
I filled myself with screaming and with water

But, my dear fellow, all that left me cold
I stayed as light and empty as before.

3
They came and battered holes right through my walls
And crawled with curses out of me again:
Nothing inside but masses of space and silence
They cursed and screamed: I must be a paper man.

4
Grinning I rolled downwards between houses
Out into the open. The grave soft wind
Now ran more swiftly through my walls
It was still snowing. Into me it rained.

5
The wretched snouts of cynical fellows have
Discovered how empty I must be.
Wild pigs have coupled in me. Ravens
Of the milky sky pissed often into me.

6
Weaker than clouds are! Lighter than the winds!
Invisible! Solemn, brutish, light
Like one of my own poems I flew through the sky
Along with a stork of somewhat faster flight!

MARY

The night when she first gave birth
Had been cold. But in later years
She quite forgot
The frost in the dingy beams and the smoking stove
And the spasms of the afterbirth towards morning.
But above all she forgot the bitter shame
Common among the poor

Of having no privacy.
That was the main reason
Why in later years it became a holiday for all
To take part in.
The shepherds' coarse chatter fell silent.
Later they turned into the Kings of the story.
The wind, which was very cold
Turned into the singing of angels.
Of the hole in the roof that let in the frost nothing remained
But the star that peeped through it.
All this was due to the vision of her son, who was easy
Fond of singing
Surrounded himself with poor folk
And was in the habit of mixing with kings
And of seeing a star above his head at night-time.

CHRISTMAS LEGEND

1
On Christmas Eve today
All of us poor people stay
Huddled in this chilly shack
The wind blows in through every crack.
Dear Jesus, come to us, now see
How sorely we have need of thee.

2
Here today we huddle tight
As the darkest heathens might
The snow falls chilly on our skin
The snow is forcing its way in.
Hush, snow, come in with us to dwell:
We were thrown out by Heaven as well.

3
The wine we're mulling is strong and old
It's good for keeping out the cold

The wine is hot, the door is shut
Some fat beast's snuffling round the hut.
Then come in, beast, out of the snow
Beasts too have nowhere warm to go.

4

We'll toss our coats on to the fire
Then we'll all be warm as the flames leap higher
Then the roof will almost catch alight
We shan't freeze to death till we're through the night.
Come in, dear wind, and be our guest
You too have neither home nor rest.

A LITURGY OF BREATH

1

An old woman appeared one day

2

Her daily bread had gone astray

3

The troops had scoffed it on the way

4

So she fell in the gutter, began to freeze

5

And there her hunger passed away.

6

At that the birds fell asleep in the trees
O'er all the treetops is quiet now
In all the hilltops hearest thou
Hardly a breath.

7
Then a coroner's assistant came that way

8
And said: the old girl must have her certificate

9
And they buried her, whose hunger was great

10
Then she had nothing more to say.

11
Just the doctor laughed at her mode of decease.

12
The birds too fell asleep in the trees
O'er all the treetops is quiet now
In all the hilltops hearest thou
Hardly a breath.

13
Then one single man came along that way

14
He'd got no sense of discipline

15
He smelled a rat and waded in

16
He stood up against her enemies

17
He said: people have to eat. Haven't they?

18

At that the birds fell asleep in the trees
O'er all the treetops is quiet now
In all the hilltops hearest thou
Hardly a breath.

19

Then all of a sudden a police inspector came that way

20

He got his rubber truncheon out

21

And battered the back of the man's head about

22

After which the man too had nothing more to say

23

But the orders the inspector bawled out were these:

24

And now all birds will fall asleep in the trees
O'er all the treetops there's to be quiet now
In all the hilltops hearest thou
Hardly a breath.

25

Then three bearded men came along that way

26

They said: this thing can't be left to one man alone

27

And went on saying so till bullets were buzzing like bees

28

But the worms crept through their flesh right into the bone

29
Then the bearded men had nothing more to say.

30
At that the birds fell asleep in the trees
O'er all the treetops is quiet now
In all the hilltops hearest thou
Hardly a breath.

31
Then all of a sudden a whole lot more men came that way

32
They wanted to speak with the troops, you see

33
But the troops spoke back with a heavy MG

34
So all those men had nothing more to say.

35
But across their foreheads ran a crease.

36
At that the birds fell asleep in the trees
O'er all the treetops is quiet now
In all the hilltops hearest thou
Hardly a breath.

37
Then one day a big red bear came that way

38
He knew nothing about the local customs, which a bear
    didn't have to obey

39
But there were no flies on him, and he wasn't born yesterday

40
And he ate up the birds in the trees.

41
Since when the birds have been squawking away
O'er all the treetops is disquiet now
In all the hilltops hearest thou
At last some breath.

III   The Impact of the Cities
1925–1928

1

I, Bertolt Brecht, came out of the black forests.
My mother moved me into the cities as I lay
Inside her body. And the coldness of the forests
Will be inside me till my dying day.

2

In the asphalt city I'm at home. From the very start
Provided with every last sacrament:
With newspapers. And tobacco. And brandy
To the end mistrustful, lazy and content.

3

I'm polite and friendly to people. I put on
A hard hat because that's what they do.
I say: they are animals with a quite peculiar smell
And I say: does it matter? I am too.

4

Before noon on my empty rocking chairs
I'll sit a woman or two, and with an untroubled eye
Look at them steadily and say to them:
Here you have someone on whom you can't rely.

5

Towards evening it's men that I gather round me
And then we address one another as 'gentlemen'.
They're resting their feet on my table tops
And say: things will get better for us. And I don't ask when.

6

In the grey light before morning the pine trees piss
And their vermin, the birds, raise their twitter and cheep.
At that hour in the city I drain my glass, then throw
The cigar butt away and worriedly go to sleep.

7

We have sat, an easy generation
In houses held to be indestructible
(Thus we built those tall boxes on the island of Manhattan
And those thin aerials that amuse the Atlantic swell).

8

Of those cities will remain what passed through them, the
        wind!
The house makes glad the eater: he clears it out.
We know that we're only tenants, provisional ones
And after us there will come: nothing worth talking about.

9

In the earthquakes to come, I very much hope
I shall keep my cigar alight, embittered or no
I, Bertolt Brecht, carried off to the asphalt cities
From the black forests inside my mother long ago.

OF THE CRUSHING IMPACT OF CITIES

But those with no hands
Without air between them
Had the strength of crude ether.
In them was constant
The power of emptiness, the greatest power of all.
They were called Lack-of-Breath, Absence, No-Shape
And they crushed like mountains of granite
That continuously fall from the air.
Oh, I saw faces
Like renegade pebbles
In swift-rinsing water
Very uniform. Many of them assembled
Formed a hole
That was very large.

Always now I am speaking
Of the strongest race only
Of the labours of the first phase.

Suddenly
Some of them fled into the air
Building upwards; others from the highest rooftops
Flung high their hats and shouted:
Next time so high!
But their successors
Fleeing from night frost after the sale of familiar roofs
Pressed on behind them and see with a haddock's eyes
Those tall boxes
Successors to houses.
For within the same walls at that time
Four generations at once
Gulped down their food
And in their childhood year
Had never seen
On a flat palm the nail for the stone in the wall.
For them metal and stone
Grew together.
So short was time
That between morning and evening
There was no noon
And already on the old familiar ground
Stood mountains of concrete.

STILL, WHEN THE AUTOMOBILE MANUFACTURER'S
EIGHTH MODEL

Still
When the automobile manufacturer's eighth model
Is already reposing on the factory scrapheap (R.I.P.)
Peasant carts from Luther's day
Stand beneath the mossy roof
Ready to travel.

Flawless.
Still, now that Nineveh is over and done with
Its Ethiopian brothers are surely ready to start.
Still new were wheel and carriage
Built for eternity the wooden shafts.

Still

The Ethiopian brother stands beneath the mossy roof
But who
Travels in it?

Already
The automobile manufacturer's eighth model
Reposes on top of the scrap iron
But we
Are travelling in the ninth
Thus we have decided
In ever new vehicles – full of flaws
Instantly destructible
Light, fragile
Innumerable –
Henceforward to travel.

OF THE REMAINS OF OLDER TIMES

Still for instance the moon
Stands above the new buildings at night
Of the things made of copper
It is
The most useless. Already
Mothers tell stories of animals
That drew cars, called horses.
True, in the conversations of continents

These no longer occur, nor their names:
Around the great new aerials
Nothing is now known
Of old times.

LITTLE EPISTLE IN WHICH CERTAIN
INCONSISTENCIES ARE REMOTELY TOUCHED ON

1
If someone enjoys writing he will be glad
If he has a subject.
When the Suez Canal was built
Someone became famous because he was against it.
There are some who write against rain
Others who are opposed to the phases of the moon.
If their piece is nicely turned
They become famous.

2
If a man lays his nose
On a railway line it
Will be carried away
When a train arrives
Irrespective of its dependability.
But it can go on lying about
Till somebody finds it.

3
The Great Wall of China, while under construction
Was opposed for two hundred years
After which it stood.

4
When the railways were young
Stage coach proprietors made snide remarks about them.
To the effect that they had no tails and ate no oats

And that you couldn't see the scenery at leisure
And who on earth had seen a locomotive's droppings
And the better they spoke
The better speakers they were.

5
As for certain grumblers
Who choose to resist laws, it's no good
Arguing with them.
It makes no impression.
Having a picture taken of them is better.
No good saying clever or complicated things to them.
Certain of my friends from the South ought to talk to them:
No splash without meaning
No vacuum with vitality
Just
Plainly.

THE THEATRE COMMUNIST

A hyacinth in his buttonhole
On the Kurfürstendamm
This youth feels
The emptiness of the world.
In the W.C. it becomes clear to him: he
Is shitting into emptiness.

Tired of work
His father's
He soils the cafés
Behind the newspapers
He smiles dangerously.
This is the man who
Is going to break up this world with his foot like
A small dry cowpat.

For 3000 marks a month
He is prepared
To put on the misery of the masses
For 100 marks a day
He displays
The injustice of the world.

I HEAR

I hear
In the markets they say of me, I sleep badly
My enemies, they say, are setting up house
My women are putting on their good clothes
In my antechamber people are waiting
Who are known to be friends of the unlucky.
Soon
You will hear that I am not eating but
Wearing new suits
But the worst is this: I myself
Notice that I have grown
Harsher to people.

SONNET

Things I remembered from those past days were
Noises of water or perhaps of trees
Outside the house; but soon I fell asleep
And lay a long time absent in her hair.

So all I know of her, by night undone
Is something of her knees, less of her neck
Her hair which smelt of bathsalts and was black
And what I'd heard about her earlier on.

They say one soon forgets her face once out of sight
Because it seems like a transparent screen
Through which nothing but emptiness is seen.

They also said her features were not bright
She knew she'd fade from people's memories
Nor would she see herself when reading this.

DISCOVERY ABOUT A YOUNG WOMAN

Next day's subdued farewell: she standing there
Cool on the threshold, coolly looked at too
When I observed a grey strand in her hair
And found I could not bring myself to go.

Silent I took her breast, and when she wondered
Why I, who'd been her guest that night in bed
Was not prepared to leave as we had said
I looked her straight between the eyes and answered:

It's only one more night that I'll be staying
But use your time; the fact is, you've provoked me
Standing poised on the threshold in that way.

And let us speed up what we've got to say
For both of us forgot that you're decaying.
With that my voice gave out, and longing choked me.

THE OPIUM SMOKER

A girl who smokes the black smoke of the evening
You know is vowed to nothingness in future.
There's nothing more can raise her up or hurt her
And two-thirds of the time she won't be living.

She can dispense with courage; she looks dreadful
(She and her hair are very nearly through)
And when she sees herself she'll wonder who
On earth that was: she's terribly forgetful.

The smoke invades her blood and fogs her wits
And so she sleeps alone: the soil is closest.
She's on the thinnest trip of her existence.

It's only others know she still exists
(She's ready for whatever won't be noticed)
She finds man's best friend, drugs, of some assistance.

COW FEEDING

Her broad chest laid against the manger railing
She feeds. Just watch that hay! She does not gulp
But mashes it awhile, the ends still trailing
Then munches carefully until it's pulp.

Her body's stout, her ancient eye is bleary
Inured to wickedness, she chews with caution.
The years have made her see things in proportion
She's not surprised now at your interfering.

And while she gets the hay down someone
Is milking her. Patient, without a sound
She lets his hand go tweaking at her teats.

She knows that hand, and doesn't turn around
She'd sooner not know what is going on
But takes advantage of the evening mood, and shits.

LOVE POEM

Waiting without a call, in his crude house
For something he can feel has started groping
Along the way towards that same crude house
About to spend its first night in the open

He checks the hut to see if it is empty –
No more lived in tomorrow than today.
To make it merely space, nothing present
Beyond himself, he puts the moon away.

But now it seems the learner's not learned right
And this first time it may have lost its bearings
He feels he too should get some sleep tonight
In case it's scared to put in an appearance.

THE GUEST

She questions him, while outside night is falling.
The tale of seven years is quickly done.
He hears them kill a chicken in the courtyard
And knows that there can only be the one.

He may not get much meat to eat tomorrow.
She says, pitch in. He says, it won't go down.
Before you came, where were you then? – In safety.
Where have you come from? – From the nearest town.

Then he stands up in haste, for time is flying.
He smiles at her, says: Fare you well. – And you?
His hand falls slowly from her. She is eyeing
The unfamiliar dust upon his shoe.

MOTHER BEIMLEN

Mother Beimlen's leg is wooden
She can walk quite naturally
With a shoe on and if we're good kids
We're allowed to look and see.

In her leg there is a cup-hook
Where she can hang her doorkey up
So as to find it even in the darkness
When she comes home from the pub.

When Mother Beimlen walks the streets and
Brings a stranger home with her
She switches the light off on the landing
And only then unlocks the door.

ON THE DEATH OF A CRIMINAL

1
He, I hear, has taken his last trip.
Once he'd cooled they laid him on the floor
Of that 'little cellar without steps'
Then things were no better than before:
That is, one of them has done the trip
Leaving us to deal with several more.

2
He, I hear, need not concern us further
That's the finish of his little game
He's no longer there to plot our murder
But alas the picture's still the same.
That is, one need not concern us further.
Leaving several more whom I could name.

OF THE COMPLAISANCE OF NATURE

Oh, the foaming milk still comes to the old man's
Slavering toothless mouth from its earthenware jug.
Oh, the dog in its search for love still fawns and cringes
Rubbing against the legs of the runaway thug.

Oh, beyond the village the elms still bow their fine branches
Gracefully to the man abusing a child
While, O murderers, the sightless kindly dust advises
How to put your blood-stained traces out of our mind.

So too the wind will mingle the screams from foundering
Ships with the rustle of leaves inland in the trees
Courteously lifting the girl's tattered hem so that
The syphilitic stranger may glimpse her delectable knees.

And at night the deep voluptuous sighs of a woman
Muffle the four-year-old in the corner whimpering with fear
While in the hand that struck the child an apple nestles
Flatteringly, off the tree that grows handsomer each year.

Oh, how the child's clear eye gets a glint in it
As Father takes out his knife and forces the ox to the ground.
And how the women heave their breasts that once suckled
        children
When troops march through the village to the band's martial
        sound.

Oh, our mothers all have their price and our sons throw
        themselves away
For the crew of the sinking ship will be glad to reach any old
        rock.
And all the dying man wants of this world is to fight, that he
May know dawn once again, and again the third crow of the
        cock.

THE GORDIAN KNOT

1

When the man from Macedaemon
Had cut through the knot
With his sword, they called him
Of an evening in Gordium, 'the slave of
His fame'.

For their knot was
One of the rare wonders of the world
Masterpiece of a man whose brain
(The most intricate in the world) had been able to leave
No memorial behind except these
Twenty cords, intricately twisted together so that they should
One day be undone by the deftest
Hands in the world – the deftest apart from his
Who had tied the knot. Oh, the man
Whose hand tied it was not
Without plans to undo it, but alas
The span of his life was only long enough
For one thing, the tying.

A second sufficed
To cut it.

Of him who cut it
Many said this was really
The luckiest stroke of his life
The cheapest, and did the least damage.

That unknown man was under no obligation
To answer with his name
For his work, which was akin
To everything godlike
But the chump who destroyed it
Was obliged as though by a higher command
To proclaim his name and show himself to a continent.

2

If that's what they said in Gordium, I say
That not everything which is difficult is useful
And an answer less often suffices to rid the world of a
    question
Than a deed.

I'M NOT SAYING ANYTHING AGAINST ALEXANDER

Timur, I hear, took the trouble to conquer the earth.
I don't understand him;
With a bit of hard liquor you can forget the earth.
I'm not saying anything against Alexander
Only
I have seen people
Who were remarkable –
Highly deserving of your admiration
For the fact that they
Were alive at all.
Great men generate too much sweat.
In all this I see just a proof
That they couldn't stand being on their own
And smoking
And drinking
And the like.
And they must be too mean-spirited
To get contentment from
Sitting by a woman.

EIGHT THOUSAND POOR PEOPLE ASSEMBLE
OUTSIDE THE CITY

'More than 8000 unemployed miners, with their wives and
children, are camping in the open on the Salgotarjan road
outside Budapest. They have spent the first two nights of their
campaign without food. They are scantily clad in rags. They
look like skeletons. If they fail to obtain food and work,
they have sworn to move on Budapest, even if this should lead
to bloodshed; they have nothing left to lose. Military
forces have been concentrated in the Budapest region, with
strict orders to use firearms if there is the slightest breach
of the peace.'

We went down to the biggest city
1,000 of us were in hungry mood
1,000 of us had had nothing to eat
1,000 of us wanted food.

The general looked from his window
You can't stop here, he said.
Go home peacefully like good chaps
If you need anything, write instead.

On the open road we halted:
'Here they'll feed us before we croak'.
But nobody took any notice
While we watched their chimneys smoke.

But the general came along then.
We thought: Here comes our meal.
The general sat on a machine gun
And what he cooked was steel.

The general said: There's too many of you bunched together
And started to count straightway.
We said: Just as many as you see here
Have had nothing to eat today.

We did not build us a shanty town
We washed no shirt again
We said: We can't wait much longer.
The general said: That's plain.

We said: But we cannot all die
The general said: Why not?
Things are warming up over there, said the people in the city
When they heard the first shot.

LEGEND OF THE UNKNOWN SOLDIER
BENEATH THE TRIUMPHAL ARCH

1
We came from the mountains and from the seven seas
To kill him.
We caught him with snares, which reached
From Moscow to the city of Marseilles.
We placed cannon to reach him
At every point to which he might run
If he saw us.

2
We gathered together for four years
Abandoned our work and stood
In the collapsing cities, calling to each other
In many languages, from the mountains to the seven seas
Telling where he was.
Then in the fourth year we killed him.

3
There were present:
Those whom he had been born to see
Standing around him in the hour of his death:
All of us.
And

A woman was present, who had given him birth
And who had said nothing when we took him away.
Let her womb be ripped out!
Amen!

4

But when we had killed him
We handled him in such a way that he lost his face
Under the marks of our fists.
This was how we made him unrecognisable
So that he should be the son of no man.

5

And we dug him out from under the metal
Carried him home to our city and
Buried him beneath stone, an arch, which is called
Triumphal Arch
Which weighed one thousand hundredweight, so that
The Unknown Soldier
Should in no circumstances stand up on Judgement Day
And unrecognisable
Walk before God
Though once more in the light
And, pointing his finger, expose us
Who can be recognised
To justice.

COAL FOR MIKE

1

I have heard that in Ohio
At the beginning of this century
A woman lived in Bidwell
Mary McCoy, widow of a railroad man
Mike McCoy by name, in poverty.

2

But every night from the thundering trains of the Wheeling
     Railroad
The brakemen threw a lump of coal
Over the picket fence into the potato patch
Shouting hoarsely in their haste:
For Mike!

3

And every night when the lump of coal for Mike
Hit the back wall of the shanty
The old woman got up, crept
Drunk with sleep into her dress and hid away the lump of coal
The brakemen's present to Mike, who was dead but
Not forgotten.

4

The reason why she got up so long before daybreak and hid
Their gifts from the sight of the world was so that
The brakemen should not get into trouble
With the Wheeling Railroad.

5

This poem is dedicated to the comrades
Of the brakeman Mike McCoy
(Whose lungs were too weak to stand
The coal trains of Ohio)
For comradeship.

THIS BABYLONIAN CONFUSION

This Babylonian confusion of words
Results from their being the language
Of men who are going down.
That we no longer understand them
Results from the fact that it is no longer

Of any use to understand them.
What use is it to tell the dead
How one might have lived
Better. Don't try to persuade
The man with rigor mortis
To perceive the world.
Don't quarrel
With the man behind whom
The gardeners are already waiting
Be patient rather.

The other day I wanted
To tell you cunningly
The story of a wheat speculator in the city of
Chicago. In the middle of what I was saying
My voice suddenly failed me
For I had
Grown aware all at once what an effort
It would cost me to tell
That story to those not yet born
But who will be born and will live
In ages quite different from ours
And, lucky devils, will simply not be able to grasp
What a wheat speculator is
Of the kind we know.

So I began to explain it to them. And mentally
I heard myself speak for seven years
But I met with
Nothing but a silent shaking of heads from all
My unborn listeners.
Then I knew that I was
Telling them about something
That a man cannot understand.

They said to me: You should have changed
Your houses or else your food

Or yourselves. Tell us, why did you not have
A blueprint, if only
In books perhaps of earlier times –
A blueprint of men, either drawn
Or described, for it seems to us
Your motive was quite base
And also quite easy to change. Almost anyone
Could have seen it was wrong, inhuman, exceptional.
Was there not some such old and
Simple model you could have gone by
In your confusion?

I said: Such models existed
But, you see, they were crisscrossed
Five times over with new marks, illegible
The blueprint altered five times to accord
With our degenerate image, so that
In those reports even our forefathers
Resembled none but ourselves.
At this they lost heart and dismissed me
With the nonchalant regrets
Of happy people.

SONG OF THE MACHINES

1
Hullo, we want to speak to America
Across the Atlantic Ocean to the great cities
Of America, hullo!
We wondered what language to speak
To make sure they
Understand us
But now we have got our singers together
Who are understood here and in America
And everywhere else in the world.

Hullo, listen to our singers singing, our black stars
Hullo, look who is singing for us . . .

The machines sing

2
Hullo, these are our singers, our black stars
They don't sing sweetly, but they sing at work
As they make your light they sing
As they make clothes, newspapers, waterpipes
Railways and lamps, stoves and records
They sing.
Hullo, now that you're all here, sing one more time
Your little number across the Atlantic Ocean
With your voice that all understand.

The machines repeat their song

> This isn't the wind in the maples, my boy
> No song to the lonely moon
> This is the wild roar of our daily toil
> We curse it and count it a boon
> For it is the voice of our cities
> It is our favourite song
> It is the language we all understand
> It will soon be the world's mother tongue.

I KNOW YOU ALL WANT ME TO CLEAR OUT

I know you all want me to clear out
I see I eat too much for you
I realise you've no means of dealing with people like me
Well, I'm not clearing out.

I told all of you flat
To hand over your meat

I followed you round and
Put it to you that you have got to move out
I learned your language for the purpose
At last
Everyone got the point
But next day there was no meat again.

I sat and waited one more day
To give you a chance to come
And put yourselves right.

When I come back
Under a rougher moon, my friends
I shall come in a tank
Talk through a gun and
Wipe you out.

Where my tank passes
Is a street
What my gun says
Is my opinion
And of the whole lot
I'll spare only my brother
By just kicking him in the teeth.

THREE HUNDRED MURDERED COOLIES REPORT
TO AN INTERNATIONAL

A dispatch from London says: '300 coolies, who had
been taken prisoner by the Chinese White Army and
were supposed to be transported to Ping Chwen in open
railway trucks, died of cold and hunger during the trip.'

1

We would like to have stayed in our villages
But they threw us out without compassion.
So we were loaded into a train like packages.
Too bad we couldn't have drawn our rice ration.

2

No covered railway trucks could be located
As they were all needed for the cattle, which can't stand the
      cold air.
Especially after our fur coats had been confiscated
We found the wind on the journey was hard to bear.

3

Again and again we asked the soldiers the reason
Why they needed us, but our guards didn't know.
They told us that if we blew on our hands it would stop us
      freezing.
They never said where we were going though.

4

The last night we halted outside a fortress wall.
When we asked when we'd get there they told us 'Some time
      today'.
That was the third day. We froze to death by nightfall.
Such times are too cold for poor people anyway.

GUIDANCE FOR THE PEOPLE ON TOP

On the day when the unknown dead soldier
Was buried amid gun salvoes
At the same midday hour
From London to Singapore
Between twelve two and twelve four
For a full two minutes, all work stopped
Simply to honour
The dead Unknown Soldier

But all the same
Perhaps instructions should be issued
For a ceremony at last to honour
The *Unknown Worker*
From the great cities on the teeming continents.

Some man from the tangle of traffic
Whose face no one noticed
Whose mysterious character was overlooked
Whose name was never heard distinctly
Such a man should
In the interest of us all
Be commemorated by a substantial ceremony
With a broadcast tribute
'To the Unknown Worker'
And
A stoppage of work by the whole of humanity
Over the entire planet.

THE GOOD NIGHT

His birth took place in great coldness
Yet it went satisfactorily none the less.
The stable they'd found in spite of all
Was warm, with moss lining the wall
And in chalk was written on the door
That *this* one was occupied and paid for.
So despite all the night was good
And the hay proved warmer than they thought it would.
Ox and ass were there to see
That everything was as it should be.
Their rack made a table, none too wide
And an ostler brought the couple a fish on the side.
And the fish was first-rate, and no one went short
And Mary teased her husband for being so distraught.
For that evening the wind, too, suddenly fell
And became less cold than usual as well.
By night time it was very nearly warm
And the stable was snug and the child full of charm.
Really they could hardly have asked for more
When the Three Kings in person turned up at the door.
Mary and Joseph were pleased for sure.

Ten Poems from a Reader
for Those who Live in Cities

I

Part from your friends at the station
Enter the city in the morning with your coat buttoned up
Look for a room, and when your friend knocks:
Do not, o do not, open the door
But
Cover your tracks.

If you meet your parents in Hamburg or elsewhere
Pass them like strangers, turn the corner, don't recognise
      them
Pull the hat they gave you over your face, and
Do not, o do not, show your face
But
Cover your tracks.

Eat the meat that's there. Don't stint yourself.
Go into any house when it rains and sit on any chair that's
      in it
But don't sit long. And don't forget your hat.
I tell you:
Cover your tracks.

Whatever you say, don't say it twice
If you find your ideas in anyone else, disown them.
The man who hasn't signed anything, who has left no picture
Who was not there, who said nothing:
How can they catch him?
Cover your tracks.

See when you come to think of dying
That no gravestone stands and betrays where you lie
With a clear inscription to denounce you
And the year of your death to give you away.
Once again:
Cover your tracks.

(That is what they taught me.)

2

We are with you in the hour when you realise
That you are the fifth wheel
And your hope goes from you.
But we
Do not yet realise it.

We note
That you drive the conversation faster
You seek the word which will let you
Make your exit
For it's a point with you
Not to attract attention.

You rise in mid-sentence
You say crossly you want to go
We say: stay! and we realise
That you're the fifth wheel.
But you sit down.

And so you sit on with us in the hour
When we realise that you are the fifth wheel
But you
No longer realise it.

You have got to be told: you are
The fifth wheel
Do not think that I who tell you
Am a villain
Don't reach for a chopper, reach
For a glass of water.

I know you no longer hear
But
Do not say loudly that the world is bad
Say it softly.

For the four wheels are not too many
But the fifth is
And the world is not bad
But
Full.

(That is something you've already heard.)

3

We do not want to leave your house
We do not want to smash the stove
We want to put the pot on the stove.
House, stove and pot can stay
And you must vanish like smoke in the sky
Which no one holds back.

If you want to cling to us we'll go away
If your woman weeps we'll pull our hats over our faces
But when they come for you we shall point
And shall say: That must be him.

We don't know what's to come, and have nothing better
But we want no more of you.
Until you've gone
Let us draw the curtains to shut out tomorrow.

The cities are allowed to change
But you are not allowed to change.
We shall argue with the stones
But you we shall kill
You must not live.
Whatever lies we are forced to believe
You must not have been.

(That is how we speak to our fathers.)

4

I know what I need.
I simply look in the glass
And see that I must
Sleep more; the man
I have is doing me no good.

If I hear myself sing, I say:
I'm gay today; that's good for
The complexion.

I take trouble to stay
Fresh and firm, but
I shan't exert myself: that
Makes wrinkles.

I've nothing to give away, but
Make do with my bit.
I eat carefully; I live

Slowly; I'm
For moderation.

(That is how I've seen people exerting themselves.)

5

I'm dirt. From myself
I can demand nothing but
Weakness, treachery and degradation
Then one day I notice
It's getting better; the wind
Fills my sail; my time has come, I can
Become better than dirt –
I began at once.

Because I was dirt I noticed
When I'm drunk I simply
Lie down and have no idea
Who is messing me about; now I don't drink any more –
I gave it up at once.

Unfortunately
Just in order to keep alive, I had to do
Much that harmed me; I've
Wolfed down poison enough
To kill four carthorses, but
What else could I do
To stay alive? So at times I sniffed snow
Till I looked
Like a boneless bedspread.
Then I saw myself in the glass –
And stopped it at once.

Of course they tried to hang a dose
Of syphilis on me, but that

Was something they couldn't manage; they could only poison
    me
With arsenic: I had
Tubes in my side with
Pus flowing night and day. Who
Would have thought that a woman like me
Would ever make men crazy again? –
I began again at once.

I have never taken a man who did not do
Something for me, and had every man
I needed. By now I'm
Almost without feeling, almost gone dry
But
I'm beginning to fill up again, I have ups and downs, but
On the whole more ups.

I still notice myself calling my enemy
An old cow, and knowing her for my enemy because
A man looks at her.
But in a year
I'll have got over it –
I've already begun to.

I'm dirt; but everything
Must serve my purpose, I'm
Coming up, I'm
Inevitable, the race of the future
Soon not dirt any more, but
The hard mortar with which
Cities are built.

(That's something I've heard a woman say.)

6

He strode down the street with his hat tipped back!
He looked each man in the eye and nodded
He paused in front of every shop window
(And everyone knows he is lost).

You ought to have heard him explain that he'd still
Got a word or two to say to his enemy
That the landlord's tone was not to his liking
That the street had not been properly swept
(His friends have already given him up).

All the same he still intends to build a house
All the same he still intends to sleep on it
All the same he still doesn't intend to rush his decision
(Oh, he's lost already, there's nothing behind him).

(That's something I've heard people say before now.)

7

Don't talk about danger!
You can't drive a tank through a man-hole:
You'll have to get out.
Better abandon your primus
You've got to see that you yourself come through.

Of course you need money
I'm not asking where you get it from
But unless you've got money you needn't bother to go.
And you can't stay here, man.
Here they know you.
If I've got you right
You want to eat a steak or two
Before you give up the race.

Leave the woman where she is.
She has two arms of her own
And two legs for that matter
(Which, sir, are no longer any affair of yours).
See that you yourself come through.

If you've got anything more to say
Say it to me, I'll forget it.
You needn't keep up appearances any longer:
There's no one here any longer to observe you.
If you come through
You'll have done more
Than anyone's obliged to.

Don't mention it.

8

Give up your dream that they will make
An exception in your case.
What your mothers told you
Binds no one.

Keep your contracts in your pockets
They will not be honoured here.

Give up your hopes that you are all destined
To finish up Chairman.
Get on with your work.
You will need to pull yourselves together
If you are to be tolerated in the kitchen.

You still have to learn the ABC.
The ABC says:
They will get you down.

Do not think about what you have to say:
You will not be asked.
There are plenty of mouths for the meal
What's needed here is mincemeat.

(Not that anyone should be discouraged by that.)

9
FOUR INVITATIONS TO A MAN
AT DIFFERENT TIMES FROM
DIFFERENT QUARTERS

There's a home for you here
There's a room for your things.
Move the furniture about to suit yourself
Tell us what you need
Here is the key
Stay here.

There's a parlour for us all
And for you a room with a bed
You can work with us in the yard
You have your own plate
Stay with us.

Here's where you're to sleep
The sheets are still clean
They've only been slept in once.
If you're fussy
Rinse your tin spoon in the bucket there
It'll be as good as new
You're welcome to stay with us.

That's the room
Hurry up, or you can also stay

The night, but that costs extra.
I shan't disturb you
By the way, I'm not ill.
You'll be as well off here as anywhere else
So you might as well stay.

10

When I speak to you
Coldly and impersonally
Using the driest words
Without looking at you
(I seemingly fail to recognise you
In your particular nature and difficulty)

I speak to you merely
Like reality itself
(Sober, not to be bribed by your particular nature
Tired of your difficulty)
Which in my view you seem not to recognise.

Poems Belonging to a Reader
for Those who Live in Cities

1

The cities were built for you. They are eager to welcome you.
The doors of the houses are wide open. The meal is
Ready on the table.

As the cities are very big
Experts have drawn maps for
Those who do not know the programme, showing clearly
The quickest way to reach
One's goal.

As nobody knew exactly what you wanted
You are of course expected to suggest improvements.
Here or there
There may be some little thing not quite to your taste
But that will be put right at once
Without your having to lift a finger.

In short, you will be
In the best possible hands. Everything is completely ready.
         All you
Need do is come.

2

Fall in! Why are you so late? Now
Just a minute! No, not you! You
Can clear out, we know *you*; it's no use your trying
To shove your way in here. Stop! Where do you think you're
         going?

Some of you there, would you be kind enough to
Hit him? That's it:
Now he's got the idea. What, still jabbering, is he?
Right, then let him have it, he's always jabbering.
Just show the fellow what it's all about.
If he imagines he can kick up a fuss over the least little thing
Hit him again, you might as well do him while you're about it.
That's it, when you've done him proper you can
Bring in what's left of him, we'll
Hold on to that.

3

The guests you see here
Have plates and cups
You
Were given a plate only
And when you asked what time the tea would be served
They said:
After the meal.

4

There are those who move half a street away
The walls are distempered after them
They are never seen again. They
Eat other bread, their women lie
Under other men, with the same sighs.
On bright fresh mornings faces and linen
Can be seen hanging from the same windows
As before.

5

Often at night I dream I can
No longer earn my living.
Nobody in this country needs
The tables I make. The fishmongers speak
Chinese.

My closest relatives
Stare at me like a stranger
The woman I slept seven years with
Greets me politely on the landing and
Passes by
Smiling.

I know
That the last room already stands empty
The furniture has been cleared away
The mattress cut to ribbons
The curtains torn down.
In short everything has been got ready
To make my unhappy face
Go pale.

The linen hanging out to dry in the yard
Is my linen; I know it well.
Looking closer however I see
Darns in it and extra patches.
It seems
I have moved out. Someone else
Is living here now and
Doing so in
My linen.

6

If you had read the papers as carefully as I do
You would have buried your hopes
That things may yet get better.

No one dies of his own accord!
And what use was the war?
True, we got rid of a few people
But how many were begotten?
And we can't even put on
A war like that every year.

What can a hurricane do?
Take the effect of two hurricanes
On Miami and all Florida:
First reports say 50,000 dead, and then
Next day it turns out to be
3,700.

You can surely replace that any day.
Even for those who live in Miami
It's a minimal relief
Let alone for us, who live
So far away from it.

It is practically an insult.
Are we now to be insulted as well?
At least we should have a right to
An undisturbed bitterness.

7

Sit down!
Are you seated?
You can lean right back.
You are to sit comfortably and at ease.

You may smoke.
It's important that you should hear me quite distinctly.
Can you hear me distinctly?
I have something to tell you which you will find of interest.

You are a flathead.
Can you really hear me?
I do hope there's no question of your not hearing me loud
      and clear?
Well:
I repeat: you are a flathead.
A flathead.
F as in Freddie, L as in Louis, A as in Annie, T as in Tommy
Head as in head.
Flathead.

Please do not interrupt me.
Don't interrupt me!
You are a flathead.
Don't say anything. No excuses!
You are a flathead.
Period.

I'm not the only one who says so.
Your respected mother has been saying it all along.
You are a flathead.
Just ask your relations
If you're not an F.
Of course no one tells you
Because you'd get vindictive, like any flathead.
But
Everyone round you has known for years you're an F.

It's characteristic that you should deny it.
That's just the point: it's characteristically F to deny it.
Oh, it's terribly hard to get a flathead to admit he's an F.
It's really exhausting.

Look, sooner or later it's got to be said
That you are an F.
It isn't entirely uninteresting to know what you are.
After all, it's a drawback not knowing what everyone knows.
Oh, you think you see things just like the other chap
But he's a flathead too.
Please don't comfort yourself that there are other Fs.
You are an F.

It's not too terrible
It won't stop you living to eighty.
In business it's a positive advantage.
And as for politics!
Invaluable!
As an F you have nothing to worry about
And you are an F.
(That's pleasant, isn't it?)

You still don't get it?
Well, who else do you want to tell you?
Brecht too says you're an F.
Come on, Brecht, give him your professional opinion.

The man's an F.
Well, then.

(This record needs to be played more than once.)

8

I told him to move out.
He'd been living in this room for seven weeks
And he wouldn't move out.
He laughed and thought
I didn't mean it.

When he came back the same night
His bags were downstairs. That
Shook him.

9

He was an easy catch.
It would have worked the second evening.
I waited till the third (and knew
It was a bit of a risk)
Afterwards he laughed and said: it's the bath salts
Not your hair.
But he was an easy catch.

For a whole month I left as soon as he'd had me.
I held off every third day.
I never wrote.
But try keeping snow in a saucepan
It turns dirty without any help.
I went on doing the best I could
Even when it was over.

I chucked out the tarts who infested his bed
As if it was part of the arrangement
I did it laughing and I did it crying.
I turned on the gas
Five minutes before he came home. I
Borrowed money in his name:
It didn't do any good.

But one night I went to sleep
And one morning I got up
Washed all over from head to foot
Ate, and said to myself:
That's that.

Actually
I slept with him twice more
But, by God and my mother
There was nothing to it.
As everything passes, so
Did that.

10

Again and again
When I look at this man
He hasn't taken a drop and
He laughs as he used to
I think: it's getting better
Spring is coming, good times are coming
The times that are gone
Have returned
Love is beginning again, soon
Things will be like they once were.

Again and again
When I've been chatting with him
He has eaten his supper and doesn't go out
He is speaking to me and
Hasn't got his hat on
I think: it will be all right
Ordinary times are over
One can talk
To a chap, he listens
Love is beginning again, soon
Things will be just like they once were.

The rain
Never falls upwards.
When the wound
Stops hurting
What hurts is
The scar

11

AN ASSERTION

Say nothing!
Which do you think changes easier
A stone, or the way you look at it?
I've always been the same.

What does a photograph signify?
A few big words
That one can prove to all and sundry?
I may not have got any better
But
I've always been the same.

You may say
I used to eat more beef
Or I got
Started quicker on the wrong track
But the best sort of unreason is the sort
That does not last, and
I've always been the same.

What does a heavy rainstorm amount to?
One or two thoughts more or less
A few emotions or none at all
Where there's not enough of everything
Nothing is enough.
I've always been the same.

12

Far be it from me to suggest that Rockefeller is a fool
But you must admit
That there was general interest in Standard Oil.

What a man it would have taken
To prevent Standard Oil from coming about!
I suggest
Such a man has yet to be born.

Who wants to prove that Rockefeller made mistakes
Since money came in anyway?
Let me tell you:
It was a matter of interest that money should come in.

You are otherwise involved?
But I would be glad to find someone
Who is not a fool, and I
Can prove it.

They picked the right man.
Didn't he have a nose for money?
Didn't he grow old?
Couldn't he do stupid things, and yet
Standard Oil came about all the same?

You think we could have had Standard Oil more cheaply
Do you suppose someone else
Could have made it come about with less effort?
(Since there was general interest?)

Are you always and everywhere against fools?
Do you think Standard Oil is a good thing?

I hope you don't believe
That a fool is
A man who thinks.

SONNET NO. 1

> In memory of Josef Klein. Beheaded for robbery
> and murder 2 July 1927 in Augsburg gaol.

I dedicate this poem to Josef Klein
It's all I can do for him, for they cut
His head off just this morning. Pity. But
That made it clear we don't approve of crime.

That's how they handle flesh and blood, the swine.
Strapped flat upon a wooden board it rode
(It got a bit of Bible that some Holy Joe'd
Picked out, well knowing that no God loves Klein).

But I think that it's really rather much.
Approve it? No, I'd really rather not
Since *their* crime never stops once they've begun it.

I don't care to be seen among that lot.
(At least not until I've had time to touch
The money that they owe me for this sonnet.)

SONNET NO. 12 (THE LOVER)

Let's face it: human flesh is prone to weakness.
Having now sampled my friend's wife's delights
I shun my room and cannot sleep at nights
But notice how I watch out for their creakings.

It's ignominious, I know. I'm sorry.
The trouble is, my room is next to theirs
Hence what he does to her reaches my ears
And if it doesn't, more's the cause to worry.

So, of an evening, when we three sit drinking
And my friend shoves the cigarettes aside
And turns his eyes towards her, damply blinking

I see to it her glass is never empty
Forcing her willy-nilly to drink plenty
That she may notice nothing in the night.

TABLET TO THE MEMORY OF 12 WORLD
CHAMPIONS

This is the story of the world middleweight champions
Their fights and careers
From the year 1891
To the present day.

I start the series in the year 1891 –
The age of crude slogging
When contests still lasted 56 or 70 rounds
And were only ended by the knockout –
With BOB FITZSIMMONS, the father of boxing technique
Holder of the world middleweight title
And of the heavyweight title (by his defeat of Jim Corbett on
        17 March 1897).
34 years of his life in the ring, beaten only six times
So greatly feared that he spent the whole of 1889
Without an opponent. It was not till the year 1914
When he was 51 that he accomplished
His two last fights:
An ageless man.
In 1905 Bob Fitzsimmons lost his title to

Jack O'Brien, known as PHILADELPHIA JACK.
Jack O'Brien started his boxing career
At the age of 18.
He contested over 200 fights. Never

Did Philadelphia Jack inquire about the purse.
His principle was
One learns by fighting
And so long as he learned he won.

Jack O'Brien's successor was
STANLEY KETCHEL
Famous for four veritable battles
Against Billy Papke
And, as the crudest fighter of all time
Shot from behind at the age of 23
On a smiling autumn day
Sitting outside his farmhouse
Undefeated.

I continue my series with
BILLY PAPKE
The first genius of in-fighting.
That was the first time people used
The term 'Human Fighting-Machine'.
In Paris in 1913
He was beaten
By a greater master of the art of in-fighting:
Frank Klaus.

FRANK KLAUS, his successor, encountered
The famous middleweights of the day
Jim Gardener, Billy Berger
Willy Lewis and Jack Dillon
And Georges Carpentier by comparison seemed weak as a
        baby.

He was beaten by GEORGE CHIP
The unknown from Oklahoma
Who performed no other deed of significance
And was beaten by

AL MCCOY, the worst middleweight champion of them all
Who was good at nothing but taking punishment
And was stripped of his title by

MIKE O'DOWD
The man with the iron chin
Beaten by

JOHNNY WILSON
Who beat 48 men K.O.
And was himself K.O.'d by

HARRY GREBB, the Human Windmill
The most dependable boxer of them all
Who never refused a contest
And fought each bout to a finish
And when he lost said:
I lost.
Who so infuriated the man-killing Dempsey
Tiger Jack, the Manassa mauler
That he flung away the gloves when training
The 'phantom who couldn't keep still'
Beaten on points in 1926 by

TIGER FLOWERS, the Negro clergyman
Who was never K.O.'d.

The next world middleweight champion
Successor to the boxing clergyman, was
MICKY WALKER, who on 30 June 1927 in London in 30
        minutes
Beat Europe's pluckiest boxer
The Scot Tommy Milligan
To smithereens.

Bob Fitzsimmons
Jack O'Brien

Stanley Ketchel
Billy Papke
Frank Klaus
George Chip
Al McCoy
Mike O'Dowd
Johnny Wilson
Harry Grebb
Tiger Flowers
Micky Walker –
These are the names of 12 men
Who were the best of their day in their line
Confirmed by hard fighting
Conducted according to the rules
Under the eyes of the world.

SONG OF A MAN IN SAN FRANCISCO

One day they all went to California
There's oil there, the papers said.
And
I too went to California.
I came out for two years.
My wife stayed in a place in the east.
My farm couldn't be kept up
But I moved to a town in the west
And the town grew when I got there.
I found no oil
I assembled cars and I thought:
The town is growing now
I'll wait till it hits 30,000.
Overnight there were many more.
Ten years go fast, when they're building houses.
I've been out ten years and I want
More. On paper
I have a wife in the east

And a roof over some faraway ground
But here
Is where the action is, and fun, and
The city's still growing.

UNDERSTANDING

I can hear you saying:
He talks of America
He understands nothing about it
He has never been there.
But believe you me
You understand me perfectly well when I talk of America
And the best thing about America is
That we understand it.

An Assyrian tablet
Is something you alone understand
(A dead business of course)
But should we not learn from people
Who have understood how
To make themselves understood?
You, my dear sir
No one understands
But one understands New York.
I tell you:
These people understand what they're doing
So they are understood.

AT POTSDAM 'UNTER DEN EICHEN'

At Potsdam *Unter den Eichen*
One noon a procession was seen
With a drum in front and a flag behind
And a coffin in between.

At Potsdam 'Under the Oak Trees'
In the ancient dusty street –
Six men were carrying a coffin
With helmet and oak leaves complete.

And on its sides in red lead paint
An inscription had been written
Whose ugly letters spelled the phrase:
'Fit for heroes to live in'.

This had been done in memory
Of any and every one
Born in the home country
Fallen before Verdun.

Once heart and soul caught by the tricks
Of the Fatherland, now given
A coffin by the Fatherland:
Fit for heroes to live in.

And so they marched through Potsdam
For the man who at Verdun fell.
Whereat the green police arrived
And beat them all to hell.

THE TENTH SONNET

I am indifferent to this world's affection.
Since my arrival tales have reached my ears
And though I'm subject to a coward's fears
The lack of greatness fills me with dejection.

A table, some great people round it, say:
I'd take the lowest place just to be there.
If fish were served, the tail could be my share
Nor, offered nothing, would I go away.

A book which made that table live for me!

And were there justice, though I practised none
I should be glad, even if I were caught.

Is all this there? Am I too blind to see?
The fact that I of all men should look down
On those in trouble hurts me to report.

CONCERNING SPRING

Long before
We swooped on oil, iron and ammonia
There was each year
A time of irresistible violent leafing of trees
We all remember
Lengthened days
Brighter sky
Change of the air
The certainly arriving Spring.
We still read in books
About this celebrated season
Yet for a long time now
Nobody has seen above our cities
The famous flocks of birds.
Spring is noticed, if at all
By people sitting in railway trains.
The plains show it
In its old clarity.
High above, it is true
There seem to be storms:
All they touch now is
Our aerials.

EVERYTHING NEW IS BETTER
THAN EVERYTHING OLD

How do I know, comrade
That a house built today
Has a purpose and is being used?
And that the brand new constructions
Which clash with the rest of the street and
Whose intent I don't know
Are such a revelation to me?

Because I know:
Everything new
Is better than everything old.

Would you not agree:
A man who puts on a clean shirt
Is a new man?
The woman who had just had a wash
Is a new woman.
New too
At all-night meetings in a smoke-filled room, the speaker
Starting a new speech.
Everything new
Is better than everything old.

In the incomplete statistics
Uncut books, factory-new machines
I see the reasons why you get up in the mornings.
The men who on a new chart
Draw a new line across a white patch
The comrades who cut the pages of a book
The happy men
Pouring the first oil into a machine
They are the ones who understand:
Everything new
Is better than everything old.

This superficial rabble, crazy for novelties
Which never wears its bootsoles out
Never reads its books to the end
Keeps forgetting its thoughts
This is the world's
Natural hope.
And even if it isn't
Everything new
Is better than everything old.

SONG OF THE CUT-PRICE POETS
(*during the first third of the twentieth century, when poetry was no
longer paid for*)

1
What you're reading now is written throughout in metre!
I say this because you no longer know (it seems)
What a poem is or what being a poet means.
Truly you might have thought up some way of treating us
     better.

2
Tell me, has nothing struck you? Do you never wonder?
Did you realise new poetry has long since ceased to appear?
And do you know why? No. Well, here's my answer:
People used to read poets once, and paid them. That's clear.

3
But no one pays out hard cash for poems today
And that's why no poetry's written now
For the poet asks not just who will read, but who'll pay
And if he's not paid he won't write. That's the pass you have
     brought things to.

4

But why should this be, he asks. Just what is my crime?
Haven't I always done what was ordered by those who paid
    us?
Whatever I promised, that I fulfilled, given time.
And now too I hear from those of my friends who are painters

5

That no more pictures are bought. Even though they say
The pictures too were flattering. Now they all remain un-
    sold . . .
So what have you got against us? Why won't you pay?
When you're getting richer and richer all the time, or so we're
    told . . .

6

Didn't we always, when we had enough to live on
Sing of the things that gave you pleasure on earth?
So they might give you pleasure anew: the flesh of your
    women
Sadness of autumn, a stream, the moon shining above . . .

7

The sweetness of your fruit, the rustle of falling leaves
And again the flesh of your women. The eternity
Round you. All this we sang, sang too your beliefs
Your thoughts of the dust you become at the end of your
    journey.

8

But this was not all you paid for, and gladly. On golden chairs
Sitting at ease, you paid for the songs which we chanted
To those less lucky. You paid us for drying their tears
And for comforting all those whom you had wounded.

9

We gave you so much. What did we ever refuse you?
Always submissive, we only asked to be paid.

What evil have we not done – for you! What evil!
And always contented ourselves with the scraps from your
        board.

10

To the shafts of your waggons sunk deep in blood and mire
Time and again we harnessed our splendid words
Called your huge slaughteryards Fields of Honour
True steel, trusty companions your bloodstained swords.

11

On the forms you sent to us demanding taxes
We painted the most astonishing pictures for you.
Bellowing in chorus our hortatory verses
The people, as always, paid the taxes you claimed were due.

12

We studied words and mixed them together like potions
Using only the strongest and best of them all.
The people swallowed everything that we gave them
And came like lambs at your call.

13

We always compared you only with what you admired
Mostly with those who, like you, received unmerited tributes
From those who, starving like us, hung round their patrons
        for food
And your enemies we hunted down with poems like daggers.

14

Why then have you all of a sudden forsaken our market?
Don't sit so long over meals! The scraps that we get will be
        cold.
Why don't you commission something – portrait or pane-
        gyric?
Or have you come to think your plain selves are a treat to
        behold?

15
Watch out! You can't dispense with us altogether!
If we could only compel you to look our way!
Believe me, sirs, today you would find our stuff cheaper.
You can't exactly expect us to give it away.

16
When I began what you're reading now (but are you?)
I wanted each stanza to rhyme all through
Then thought: That's too much work. Who'll pay me for it?
And so regretfully left it. It'll just have to do.